PROJECTS *from the* MINIMALIST WOODWORKER

For Paprika, who always helps to carry the other end of the board—no matter how heavy.

Publisher & Editor: Matthew Teague
Copy Editor: Megan Fitzpatrick
Design & Layout: Lindsay Hess
Photography: Vic Tesolin
Index: Jay Kreider

Blue Hills Press
P.O. Box 239
Whites Creek, TN 37189

ISBN: 978-1-951217-25-9
e-book ISBN: 978-1-951217-31-0

Library of Congress Control Number: 2021933275

Printed in the United States
10 9 8 7 6 5 4 3 2 1

To learn more about Blue Hills Press books, or to find a retailer near you, email info@bluehillspress.com or visit us at www.bluehillspress.com.

PROJECTS *from the* MINIMALIST WOODWORKER

BUILDING TECHNIQUES *for* MASTERING ESSENTIAL TOOLS

VIC TESOLIN

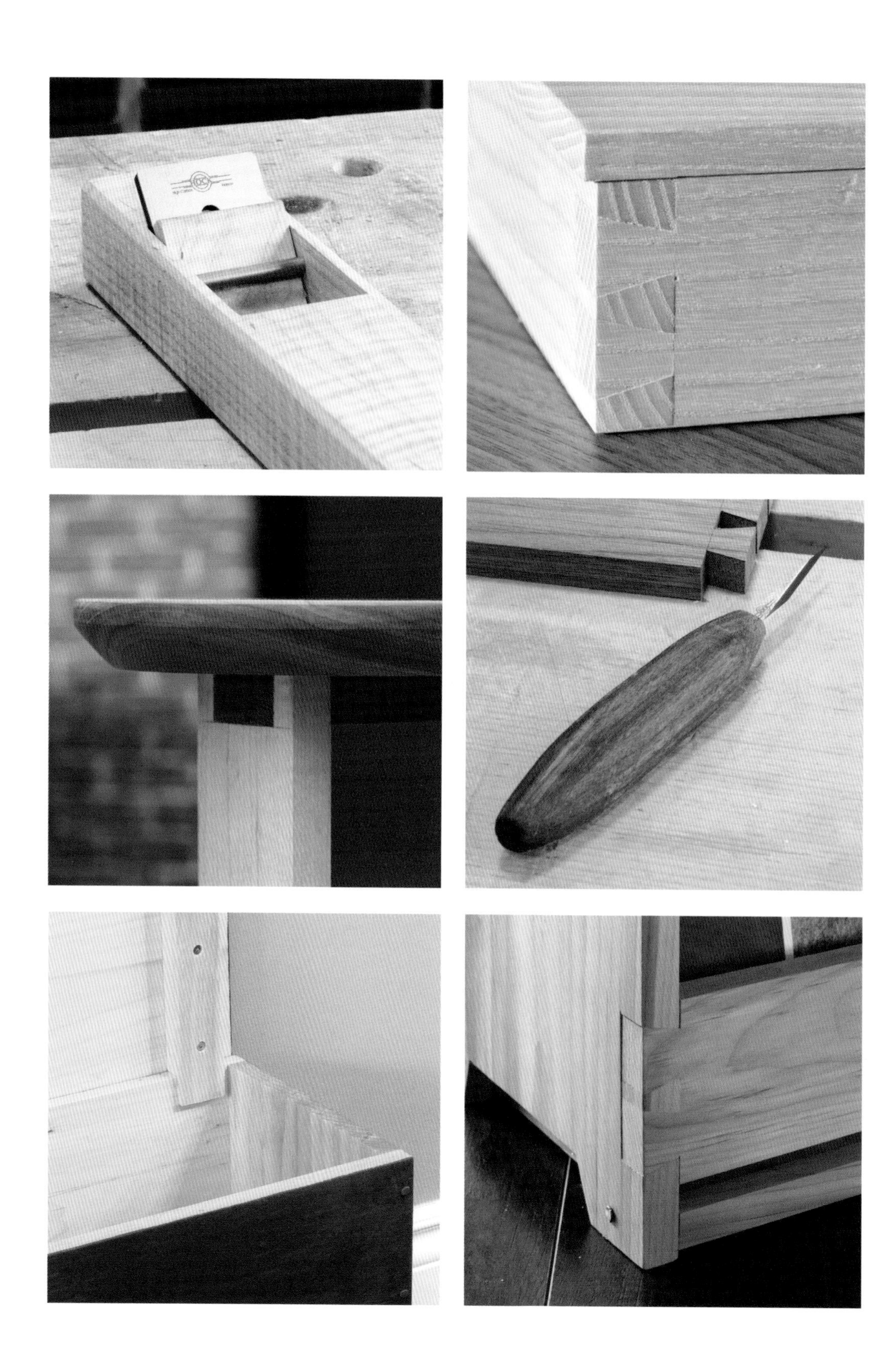

CONTENTS

FOREWORD: 6

INTRODUCTION: 8

10
VIOLIN KNIFE

22
WOODEN PLANE

36
DOVETAILED BOX

56
PERCH STOOL

82
ALBUM CRATE

102
6-BOARD CHEST

124
HANGING WALL CABINET

INDEX: 158

FOREWORD

BY STEVE DER-GARABEDIAN

In order to understand, you must do. Those are not my words but rather Vic Tesolin's. I think it says a lot about him and his philosophy. It's a very practical way of approaching things not only in woodworking but in life. You can hum and haw about this technique or that project, but better yet, just do.

As I was growing up, my mother impressed upon me that it's not the monetary value of a person that shows they are wealthy, rather it's the company that they keep. I'm richer in life for having Vic as a friend, a brother, someone to bounce ideas off—and also to help carry heavy table saws down to basement workshops. I mean really heavy. "We won't do that again" kind of heavy. We both attended Rosewood Studio years ago and that gave us good bones for the structure of our woodworking careers. Education is a great thing; what you do with it after all the lessons are over might very well be the truest measuring stick. Whether that stick is metric or imperial is your choice.

A number of years ago Vic had a brilliant idea that we should teach together at the circuit of woodworking shows here in eastern Canada. We are the Vic and Steve show and I'm proud of what we've accomplished so far. We have a lot of fun and still manage to teach a thing or two. People have said that they're reminded of Penn and Teller, however, neither one of us is silent, though I like to think we do a bit of magic with wood.

As I stand beside Vic at the shows while he demonstrates, I'm blown away by some of the tips and tricks he comes up with. It pushes me to do better. It pushes me to get out of what always works for me and experiment to see if this method might be better or a particular finishing technique might shine above others or if my shop layout could use a bit of a shuffle.

It's very pleasing to see how Vic starts with an idea, then executes it. He's not afraid to try things to see if they work better. He tries them in order to understand. You the reader, the worker of wood, get this in the form of his now second

Approaching our craft in a minimalist manner brings us back to what really counts.

book. There doesn't seem to be any hesitation, either, once he's thought something through. Yes, a measurement might have to be changed or a new angle might have to be brought in, but Vic wouldn't know this if he didn't try it.

What does this mean as far as you're concerned? While there are a lot of us, the woodworking community is a rather small group in the big scheme of things. Sharing your knowledge with other people is one of the most noble things you can do. It's how we grow. Vic brings a lot to the workbench with his wealth of experience. You're going to learn new techniques and skills if you're just starting out, or pick up a new way of doing things that just might be better than what you've tried so far.

Tools in the latest catalogs sometimes get in the way of what the real purpose behind them is. Is it about the tool you buy or what you're supposed to make with it? Do we really need the latest and greatest? Will a laser really make a difference? There is always going to be another new-and-improved version to help you part with your hard-earned dollars. There is no measuring device that I know of that can calculate the satisfaction of making a tool yourself to use for an upcoming project. Don't lose track of why we pick up a piece of wood. Approaching our craft in a minimalist manner brings us back to what really counts. The first is that it should provide something useful. A cabinet to store spices, a box for precious items, or perhaps a stool to perch on. Second, possibly the more important of the two, it should be fun. Don't worry about cutting dovetails faster. If you make a mistake building a piece, put it in your shop and use it as a lesson. It is perfectly fine to not finish every project this weekend.

Vic pushes me to be better and to try things in a different way. (With one exception: I'm still going to cut my dovetails pins first.) I've seen the projects you're going to read about and make. I'm going to be making them as well.

INTRODUCTION

Here we are again. Book number two on the use of hand tools in a small shop. I hope by now I've been able to convince you that you don't need a ton o space with a bunch of power tools in order to create wooden projects. Of course, there are many advantages to using power tools if you have the room and budget for them. The reality, however, is that you don't need them in order to work wood. I like to think of machines as apprentices—not essential but they can be nice to have. They can take on drudgery tasks such as dimensioning stock or creating multiple parts. In the first book we talked all about the tools that you need and how to keep those tools sharp. We then went through the construction of some of the more critical pieces of shop furniture, appliances, and tools to get you started. Now it's time to step up our game a bit and look at some more advanced techniques.

In this book we are going to add a couple more tools to your tool kit including a wooden plane that blends the best of both Eastern and Western woodworking traditions, along with a small shop knife that I would be lost without. The projects in this book were selected and designed to have a certain duality to them. If you're happy with how the project turns out, you can include it somewhere in your home. However, if you learned some valuable lessons but don't care to feature a particular piece in your house, use the project in your shop.

The remainder of the projects will introduce new techniques including cutting dovetails (both decorative and functional), working with veneer, cutting mortise-and-tenon joints, and so much more! I continue to learn new techniques as I progress through this craft and so will you. Learning new processes is necessary for growth and increases your options for both design and joinery.

You'll note in the photos that my bench looks a little different from the first book. I have added a Record vise to the front of my bench because I already had it and it does offer a certain amount of convenience. Adding a vise to this style of bench is pretty simple, and you will find many videos on YouTube on how to complete this task. Like machines, a vise is not required in order to work wood, but it can make things a bit easier.

While I've maintained the use of hand tools only, you'll also see that I've incorporated a few that work on more than human power. In this book I use a small cordless drill instead of an eggbeater-style hand drill. I find the cordless drill to be a ubiquitous tool that is relatively quiet and available at many price points. The nice feature of this style is that you only need one hand to operate it, leaving your other hand available to hold things. I will also mention that a small drill press is a handy tool for some of the projects in this book, but it is certainly not necessary. When you are required to drill a hole for woodworking, the hole often needs to be a specific size and angle. A drill press (even a small one) can be very helpful in achieving that accuracy. Fear not though, I outline other ways to drill accurately using simple jigs, so please don't feel that you have to run out and buy a drill or drill press.

Woodworking is all about versatility, exploration, and learning. Minimalist woodworking is about making woodworking accessible and enjoyable to all. How we each define minimalism may differ, but at the end of the day, it's about what works for you.

So, I'll keep this short and sweet: We've got a lot of stuff to make, so let's get on with it!

In order to understand, you must do.

Vic Tesolin

CHAPTER 1

VIOLIN KNIFE

There are certain tools that I own that I couldn't be without, and the violin knife is one of them. While I have never built a violin (nor intend to), the shape and size of this knife is perfect for all sorts of general woodworking tasks. I use mine for tasks like paring, carving, and trimming, but where it really helps me out is when dovetailing. This knife is slender and can slip into all kinds of tight spots, and is perfect for cleaning out the crumbly bits of wood in the corners of the tails and pins.

Ron Hock of Hock Tools makes fantastic knife blanks from high-carbon steel, so the only thing left for you to do is make a handle. You don't need much wood for this project, and you can likely find a small bit of wood in your scrap pile. You can also head to your local wood seller and check out the turning blanks for a suitable small piece. This could even be an opportunity to try out a bit of exotic wood, but be aware that sometimes the most beautiful piece of wood can be a real bear to work with hand tools. You've been warned.

TOOLS

Ruler
Marking gauge
Rip panel saw
Smoothing plane
Marking knife
Chisels
Mallet
Router plane
Coping saw
Rasps and files
Sandpaper
Spokeshave (optional)

MATERIALS

5-minute epoxy
Masking tape

CUT LIST

PART	LENGTH	WIDTH	THICKNESS
Handle blank	7"	1"	1"
Hock knife blade (VK075)			

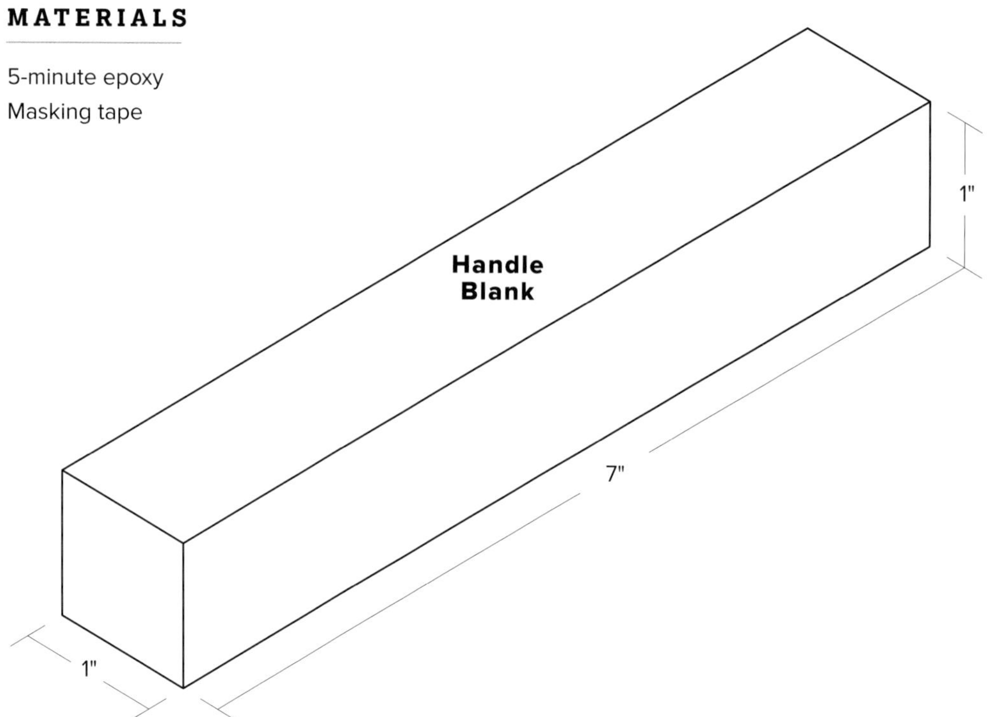

PREPARE THE WOOD BLANK

1 | Start Square. The blank should be 1" square and the length of the knife blank. This will ensure that you have extra material at the end of the knife to shape without exposing the metal.

2 | X Marks the spot. Locate the center of the blank's end by drawing lines from corner to corner to locate the center of the blank. Then use a marking gauge set to half the thickness of the knife blade and mark a line next to the centerline. Carry this line all the way around the blank.

3 | Cut to the line. Begin resawing the blank on the line you just struck.

SPLIT THE BLANK IN HALF

4 | Cut along the length. Start sawing in from the ends of the blank until the back of the saw stops you. Then lay the blank on its side and connect the two kerfs with the saw. This will yield two parts—one slightly wider than the other.

5 | Keep the halves aligned. Mark a cabinetmaker's triangle on the two pieces so that when you put them back together it will look like one piece of wood.

6 | Smooth the rough faces. Now clean up the saw marks with a small smoothing plane to create two surfaces that will glue together seamlessly.

MORTISE FOR THE BLADE

8

7 **Mark the location.** Lay the knife blank onto the thicker of the two halves of wood. There's no need to measure here. Trust your eye to get it located in the center; if it's a bit off-center, it's not the end of world. Use another knife to mark the location of the knife blade on the end of the handle blank.

8 **Cut lines are easy to follow.** Use a marking gauge to carry the lines down the length of the blank.

9 **Locate the blade end.** Then use the knife to mark in the end of the knife blank.

MORTISE FOR THE BLADE *(continued)*

10 | Start removing waste. You've marked a groove for the knife blank to rest in and now you need to muck it out. Pick a chisel that is a bit smaller than the width of groove you've marked. Begin by making a row of cuts across the grain within the knife lines. This will begin to rough out the groove. Take your time with this so that you stay between the lines. Like coloring, you don't want to go outside the lines because you will end up with a sloppy groove.

11 | Knock off the loose ends. To remove the first bit of waste you can turn your chisel perpendicular to the groove and rub the back of the chisel along the surface. The small bits of waste should start to lift out, starting the groove.

12 | Set up the router plane. Set the cutter on your router plane to the thickness of the knife blank. To do this, simply zero the blade on a flat surface then trap the blade blank between the stop and the body of the plane. Then let the stop drop into the plane's body, and lock the blade in place.

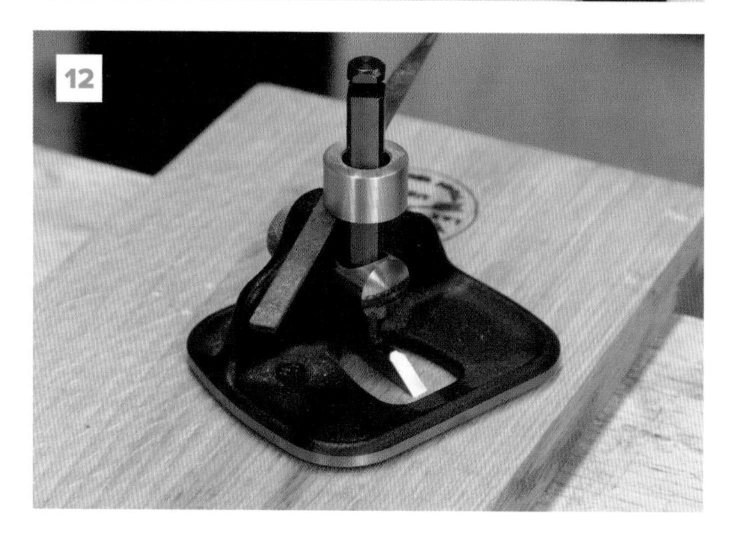

13 | Work slow and sure. If your router doesn't have a stop, don't panic. Just take progressively deeper cuts and test the depth with the knife blank after each pass to ensure you don't go too far.

You can probably see why I prefer a smaller router for this operation, but a full-size router will do the trick as well. Just be careful to keep the tool balanced on the blank.

14 | Clean up the mortise. Keep going until the blade blank sits flush in the groove you've made. It's okay if the blank is a whisper below the surface but it cannot be proud because the two halves of the handle won't come together if it is.

GLUE THE BLADE IN PLACE

15 | **Put epoxy in the groove.** It's now time to make these two pieces of wood one again. Before you get too far down this path, indicate on the outside of the handle where the blade ends. This will save you from trying to saw through metal with you best saw. For bonding metal and wood, I prefer 5-minute epoxy. You can use regular epoxy but this project doesn't really need the added strength. 5-minute epoxy comes in two parts: resin and hardener. Follow the directions on the package and remember you have five minutes before it sets up so work with some urgency, but don't rush. You should also wear gloves because epoxy tends to make a sticky mess everywhere. Apply epoxy into the groove and on the adjacent surface. No need to go heavy on the epoxy as most of it will just end up as squeeze-out, adding to the mess.

16 | **Clamp it up.** Align the two halves using the cabinetmaker's marks and clamp the assembly together. Once the clamps are set, wipe off the excess epoxy, especially at the top end. Otherwise you will end up with blobs of epoxy stuck to the blade. While doing that, be mindful of the sharp bit of steel sticking out of the handle. Keep the excess epoxy close at hand so that you can monitor the curing process. Once the stuff in the cup goes off, you're good to remove the clamps.

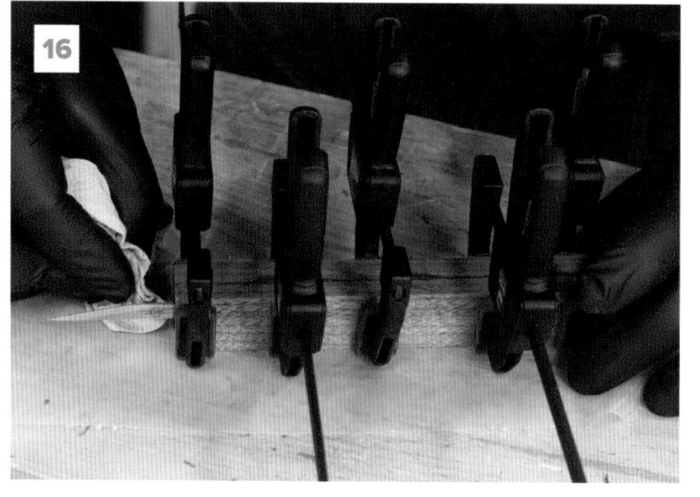

SHAPE THE HANDLE

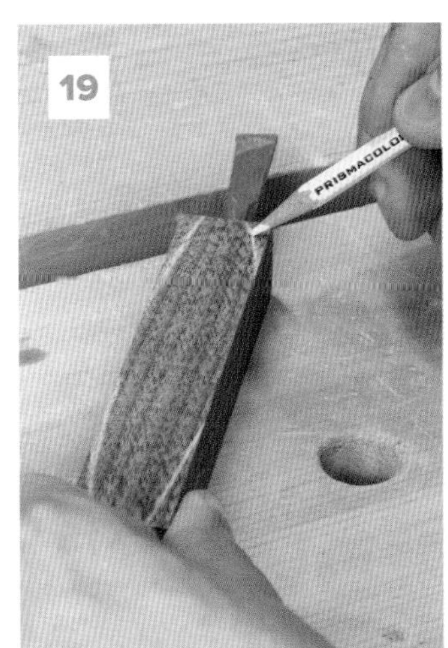

17 | Protect the blade. Now we get to the fun part—shaping. Start by wrapping that sharp, pointy blade in some masking tape. This will save you from getting cut, but more important, from wrecking the sharp blade while shaping the handle. The shape you choose for your knife is really up to you. I've used a few different knives over the years and know what I like, but make it comfortable for you and your hand.

18 | Cut it to length. Start by removing the extra wood at the end and remember to spot that mark you made for where the blade ends inside.

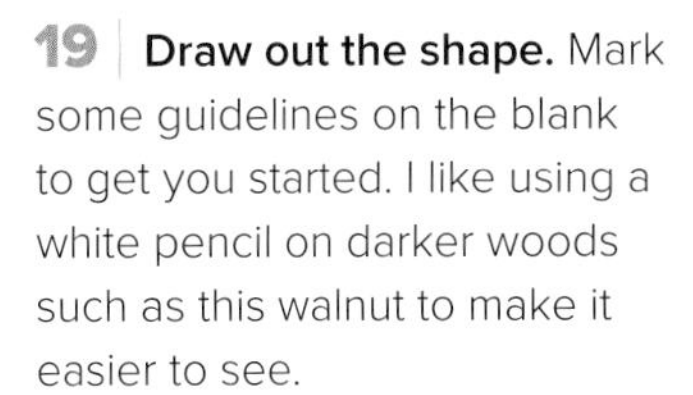

19 | Draw out the shape. Mark some guidelines on the blank to get you started. I like using a white pencil on darker woods such as this walnut to make it easier to see.

20 | Cut away what you can. Start off by removing the bulk of the waste with a coping saw or bow saw. Keep your lines at this point—you can always take more off but it's harder to put material on.

REFINE THE SHAPE

21 **Start with a spokeshave.** Now you can start to whittle away at what's left. A spoke-shave with a single-handed grip is a great way to do this because it's like using a carving knife with the helpful addition of sole.

22 **Adjust as you work.** You can use a number of grips on the spokeshave to shape the different parts of the handle. There is no easy way to hold the knife handle in a vise while you shape so using the shave one-handed is a great option.

21

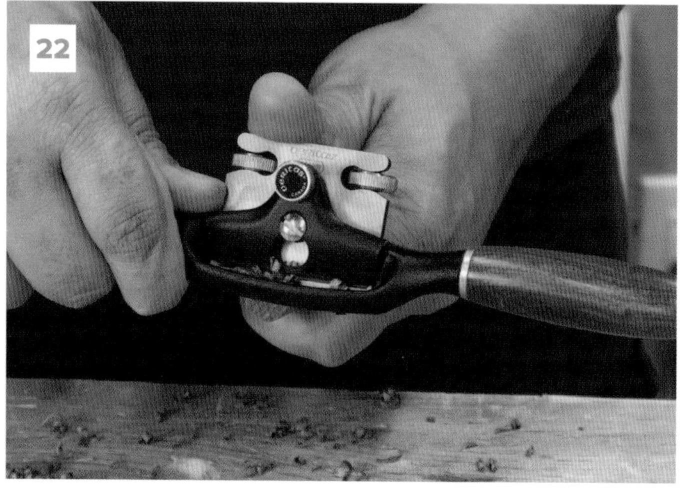
22

23 | **Smooth it out.** Once the shape is roughed in, switch to a fine rasp to further refine the shape and remove the facets that the spokeshave left behind. Of course, if you don't have a spokeshave, you can use a rasp to shape the handle start to finish. I use the dog holes in my bench as a work-holding solution and because the bench is made from soft-wood, I don't have to worry about denting the walnut. You may not get away with this trick if you have a benchtop made from hardwood.

24 | **Finish it off.** I don't go any further with the shaping of the handle because I like the texture left by the rasp. It feels good in the hand and the texture makes it stay put as you use it. You can certainly smooth it out further with sandpaper, but the I find that knives with a super-smooth finish slip in the hand during use—not really what you want. You can use an oil finish or wax on this tool but, again, I wouldn't go too crazy with the finish. I like to feel the wood of the handle as I use it. Over the years it will become a welcome feeling in your hand and will help you finesse joinery and shapes for a long time.

HOCK
High Carbon
France

CHAPTER 2

WOODEN PLANE

I feel a certain pride when I practice my craft using tools I made myself. These tools are the most treasured in my shop because they were made by me, for me. And I especially like wooden smoothers because I love the surface they create. The wooden body of the plane burnishes the surface of the workpiece, creating a more lustrous surface. This plane was designed to be pulled (as with Japanese woodworking) or pushed, depending on the situation. Most sandwich-style planes require material larger than 8/4 thick but this one requires only 8/4 stock, which is easier to find. In this example I use curly maple, which is stable and works well with hand tools. I've seen many planes made of exotic timbers, but woods indigenous to North America are usually easier to work with hand tools.

The blade for this plane is a Hock blade originally designed to use in making Krenovian planes. When you buy this blade it comes with a chipbreaker. I've chosen not to use a chipbreaker because I don't feel that the plane needs it. You can use other 2" blades that you may have on hand, but keep in mind that the blade's thickness will require you to change the thickness of the wedge to accommodate the difference.

TOOLS

- Marking gauge
- Rip panel saw
- Crosscut saw
- Jack plane
- Block plane
- Sandpaper
- Clamps
- 6" flat mill file
- Plane float (optional)

MATERIALS

- PVA glue
- Brass pin, ¼" diameter

CUT LIST

PART	LENGTH	WIDTH	THICKNESS
Plane blank	12"	4"	1-¾"
Brass rod	3"	¼" diameter	
Hock blade (PI200)	3½"	2"	

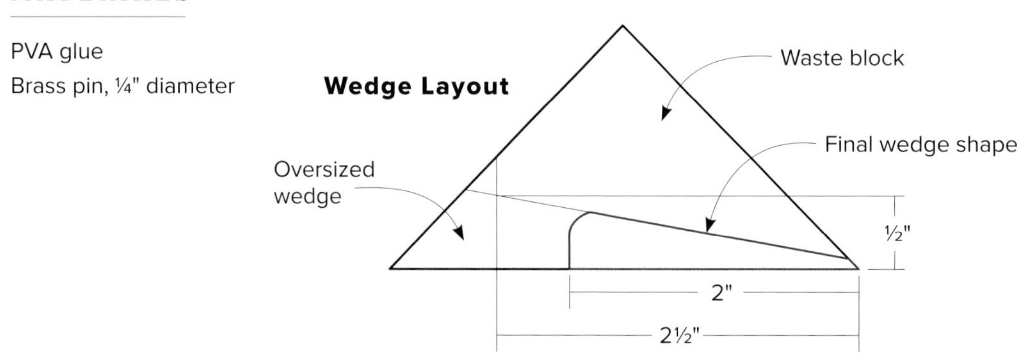

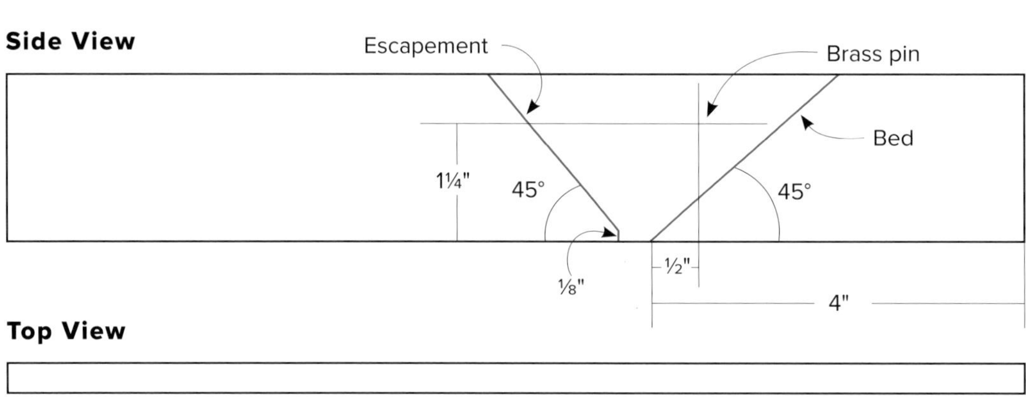

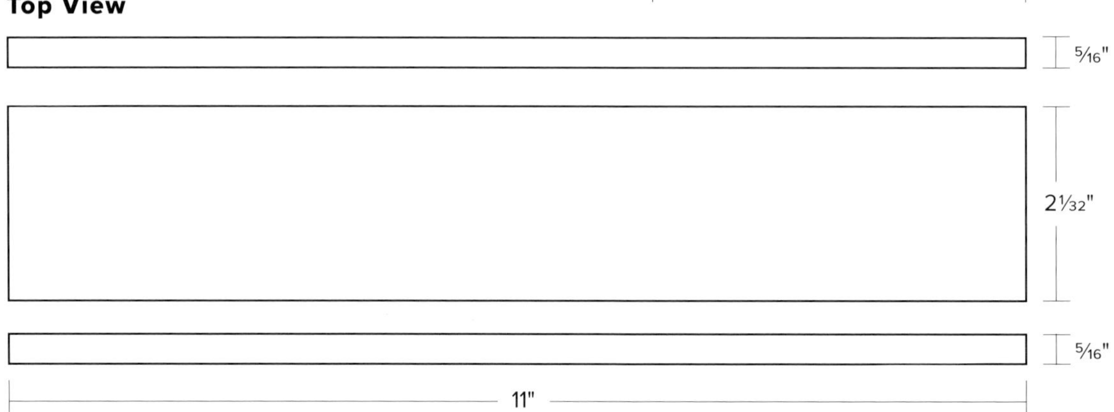

PREP & CUT THE PARTS

1 **Square up the blank.** The finished plane is made from four parts: two cheeks, the front core, and the rear core. The rear core will be the bed, the front core will create the space for the escapement, and the cheeks hold the whole thing together. All of these parts are cut from a single blank. Start by cutting and smoothing the blank according to the cut list. The blank size allows room for saw kerfs and planning, so don't panic if it seems large.

Bring the blank to 4-square, not worrying about the length at this time. Working accurately from the start is critical so that you aren't fighting with layout later. It also bears mentioning that the blank should be oriented so that you are pulling the plane with the grain of the plane rather than against. This prevents fibers from the plane's sole from being lifted or ripped off during planing. Mark the blank with a cabinetmaker's triangle to help keep parts sorted.

2 **Mark the cheek location.** Set a marking gauge to 5⁄16" and strike a line down the length of the blank and all the way around.

3 **Go easy on the eyes.** You can also darken the knife lines with a pencil to make them easier to see.

BREAK THE BLANK INTO PARTS

4 | Cut away the cheek. Secure the blank to your bench and begin ripping off what will become the first cheek of the plane. Put the kerf of your saw to the outside of your layout lines, wasting the cut in the cheeks. Take your time with the cuts and let the saw do the work, as the old adage says. If you like, take a scrap piece of wood similar in size and practice sawing before you go for it. Saw halfway through the blank then rotate it 180° and saw in from the other end, meeting in the center.

5 | Smooth it out. Once the first cheek is sawn, clean up the blank of the saw marks and be sure to keep the blank square as you work.

6 | Mark the blade location. Lay the blade down on the blank, add 1⁄32" to the width and make a pencil mark.

Carry the line down the surface and around the blank. Saw out the core piece as you did the first cheek. It's critical that the blank end up no narrower than 2-1⁄32". Otherwise the blade will not have enough room to be adjusted laterally.

4

5

6

7

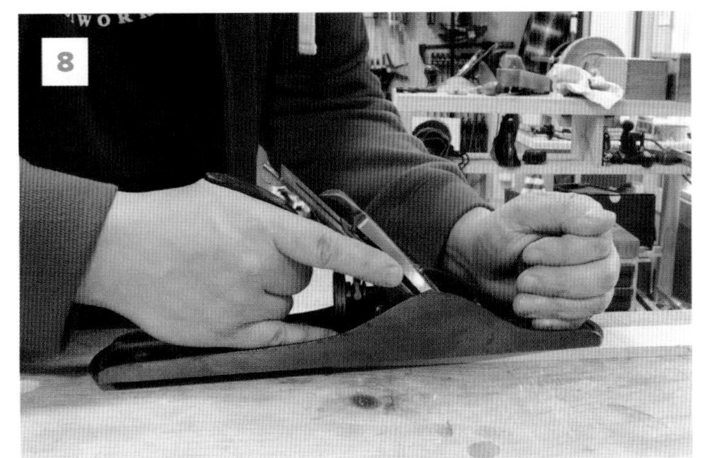
8

9

10

7 Keep parts aligned. The inside surfaces need to be clean and flat to get a good glue-up.

8 Clean up the faces. Use a jack plane to create this flat surface on the two cheek pieces, then turn your attention to the core piece.

9 Mark out the core. With the core dimensioned and square, it's time to lay out the bed and escapement. Reference the drawing on p. 24 for the dimensions. Both the bed and the escapement are 45°. I always like to have those two dimensions add up to 90° regardless of what the bed angle is because I find it gives ample room to get fingers in there to clear shavings.

10 Cut to the lines. I use a crosscut kataba saw and a saw guide to help with the cut. You could also use a miter box, but I highly recommend you use some sort of bench aid to make this cut. It is critical that the bed be square to the side of the core and using one of these options will get you close, leaving a bit of truing with a block plane. Simply set the saw guide on the line you marked and clamp it to the block. Go easy with these cuts and again, let the saw cut. Forcing the saw will only jam up the gullets between the teeth and cause the cut to run afoul.

11 | **Keep your parts organized.** You may be surprised by how clean the cut is if you take your time, requiring little truing with the plane. Don't get rid of the triangle of waste you've created; you'll need it later.

12 | **True up the bed.** Take fine cuts with a block plane and work methodically so that you don't remove too much material. It's physically easier to take light cuts with the block plane and it will save you from chasing square as a result of being too heavy handed.

13 | **Square the faces.** Once both core pieces are true, create a flat facet perpendicular to the sole of the plane on both pieces. The rear core only requires about a 1⁄32" facet to prevent that edge from catching the work.

14 | **Facet the front.** The front core will take a 1⁄8" facet to prevent the mouth from growing in size from the flattening process. You will likely have to flatten your plane a couple of times a year; thankfully, it's easy to do.

11

12

13

14

PUT IT BACK TOGETHER

15 | Take a test run. It's now time to glue the four parts of the plane together. Start by tidying up your bench and laying down some paper to catch any glue. I have a scrap of melamine that I like doing glue-ups on because it's flat and the glue cleans up easily from the surface. I also lay out all of the clamps that I need and do a dry glue-up first to make sure everything comes together as planned. This also lets me know if I have enough clamps for the task instead of running around finding clamps while the glue is setting up. When using parallel jaw clamps as I've done here, you don't need to use clamping cauls. However, if you're using F-style clamps, some cauls will help disperse the clamping pressure.

16 | Lay on the glue. Apply an even coat of glue on all of the core pieces. Remove the glue from the margin adjacent to the escapement area to prevent an excess of glue squeeze-out.

17 | Check your fit. Align and clamp the parts loosely, insert the blade and tighten the rear clamps a bit more then turn your attention to the front of the plane. Slide the front core piece to meet the blade so that the blade cannot slide though the body, then clamp in place. You will be opening the mouth to allow the blade through in a later step.

PUT IT BACK TOGETHER *(continued)*

18 | Position your clamps. Be sure that parts remain flat referencing the sole and don't worry about the cheek alignment. We will trim those flush later.

19 & 20 | Apply even pressure. Go around the plane tightening clamps as required. Then remove the blade and let the glue do its thing.

21 | Clean it up. Take a moment with a damp cloth to remove as much squeeze-out as you can. Once the glue is dry, remove the plane from the clamps and inspect the interior surfaces for any rogue glue and remove it with a sharp chisel. Gently scrape away any hard glue left on the top and sole of the plane, then trim the ends flush and to final dimension.

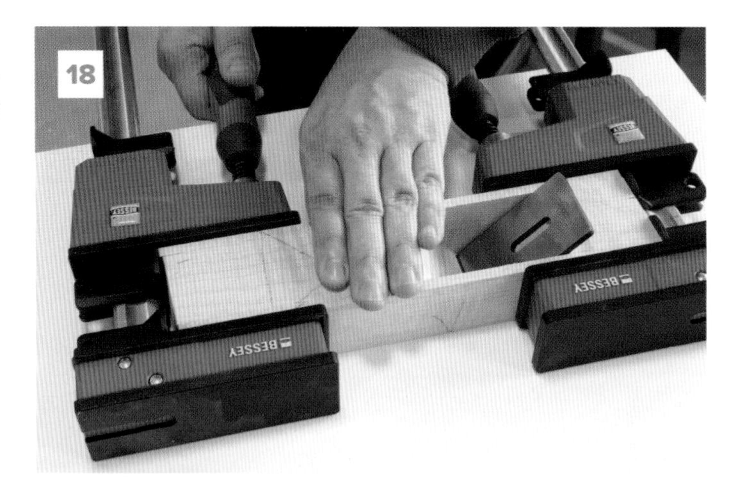

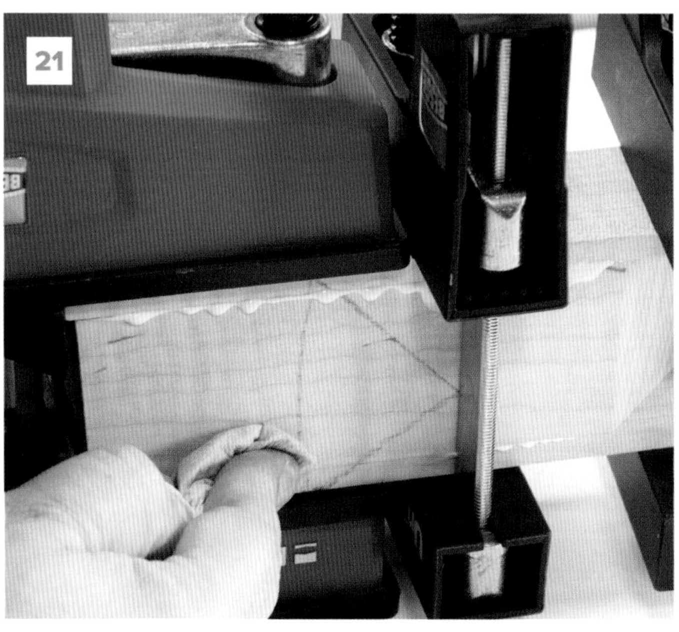

DRILL OUT FOR THE PIN

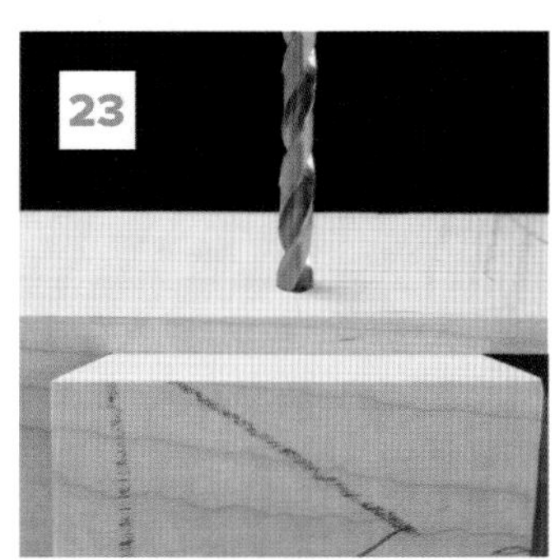

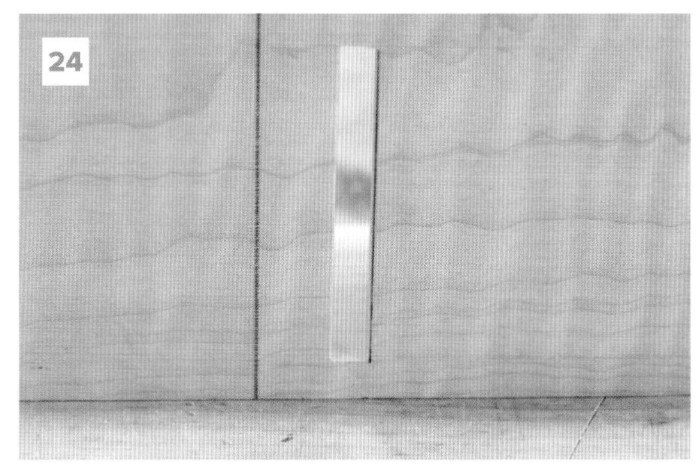

22 | Locate the hole locations. Use the drawing on p. 24 as a guide. Take your time—any misalignment will lead to a pin that isn't straight (and more difficult to fit).

23 | Drill it out. Insert the waste block into the escapement area to back up the drilling so that you get a clean exit hole on the inside surfaces. Drill the hole as straight as possible and only bore down until you hit the waste block, then repeat these steps for the other side. Again, save that waste block; it will become the stock for your wedge!

24 | Prepare for the blade. To open the mouth, start by marking a gauge line parallel to the front of the mouth opening. This will serve as a visual gauge to keep your filing in check. I like to use ink for this line because it is easier to see. Pick a small, flat file or float to slowly open the mouth.

25 | Open up the mouth. Be mindful of the file's position, focusing on keeping it perpendicular to the sole. Remove a bit of material then test with the blade to gauge your progress. The mouth should only be open a whisper for a fine smoother and can be much wider if the tool will be used for rougher tasks like mass stock removal.

CREATE & INSTALL THE WEDGE

26 | Draw out the wedge. Move on to making the wedge. Lay it out on the waste piece according to the drawing on p. 24. Carry the lines all the way around the block.

27 | Cut it to shape. Saw to the lines but don't remove them. It is best to leave the wedge a bit oversized so that you can sneak up on the fit.

28 | Square up the wedge. With that in mind, reduce the width of the wedge to match the width of the blade. This will make it easier to judge the blade's position in the body I built a small shooting board that uses my block plane for smaller tasks like squaring and cleaning up the wedge.

29 | Smooth the face. The same shooting board can be used to hold the wedge as you smooth the face.

30 Install the pin and wedge. To cut the brass pin to length, a hacksaw or any metal cutting saw works fine. Then slide the ¼" brass pin into place. I usually don't adhere the pin into plane, but if you don't have enough friction to hold it you can secure it with a bit of 5-minute epoxy.

Leave the wedge longer than required as you fit it in place. The extra length will make it much easier to get it in and out of the plane. Insert the blade into the plane then attempt to seat the wedge. A few gentle taps with a plane-adjusting hammer will force the wedge into place. Remove the wedge and inspect the top surface of it. You should see burnishing marks (shiny areas) left by the pin. These marks are your guide to where you need to remove material in order to fit the wedge. Ultimately you want the wedge to be burnished across its entire width so remove only the shiny areas with a block plane. The goal is to get the wedge to seat so that the leading edge of it extends ½" to ¾" below the pin.

31 Fine-tune the wedge. With the wedge fitting well, you can now trim off the extra length with a saw and shape the wedge with a block plane according to the drawings.

REFINE THE SHAPE OF THE PLANE

32 | Shape the body of the plane. You can now move on to flattening the sole and the finishing work. Create chamfers about 3⁄16" wide on all the edges including the sole with a block plane. To mimic the pressures of everyday use, it's best to flatten the plane with the blade and wedge in place. Install the blade and set the wedge, ensuring the blade is retracted above the sole of the plane.

33 | Keep track of your work. Drawing pencil marks across the sole of the plane enables you to gauge your progress when flattening it.

34 | Flatten the sole. Attach adhesive-backed sandpaper to a flat surface and pull the plane along the sandpaper to flatten the sole.

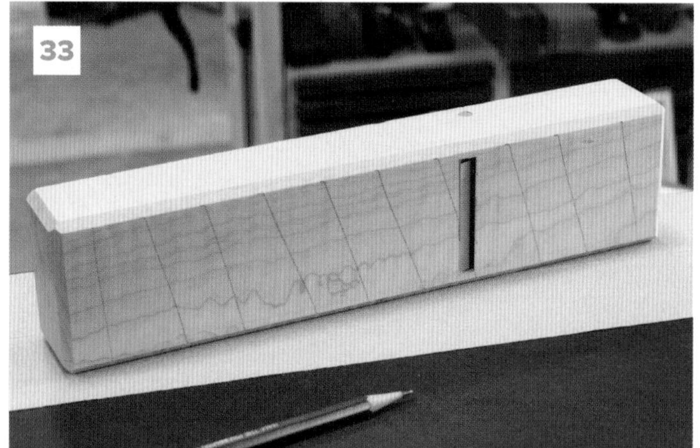

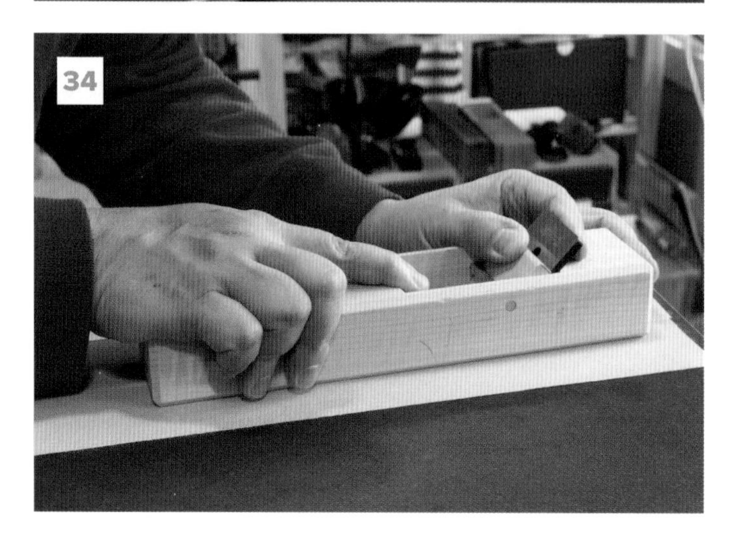

FINISH IT OFF

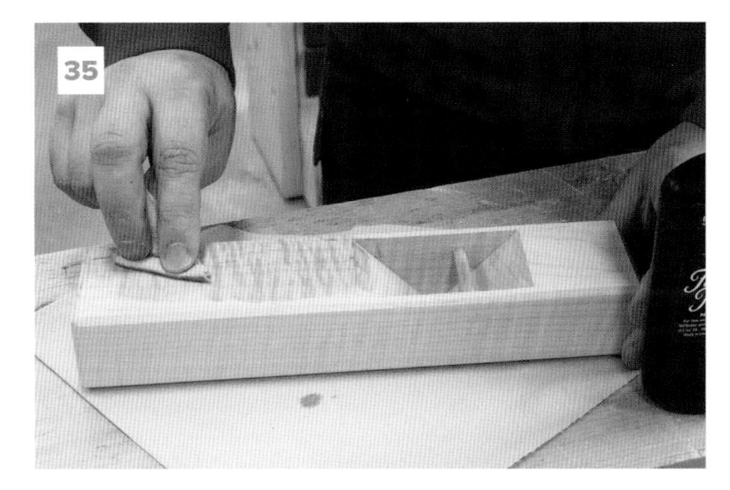

35 **Lay on the finish.** I prefer a light coat of wax or a single coat of oil, such as boiled linseed, on my tools because I like to feel the wood rather than a candy-coated finish, but you can use whatever you like.

36 **Install the blade.** Set up the plane by starting with the blade just above the sole with the wedge tapped in to secure it. Then pull the plane toward yourself while gently tapping the blade deeper into the plane body. If you listen carefully you should hear the blade sliding against the wood before it makes a shaving. At this point tap the wedge tighter and take a test cut. If the blade is cutting askew, tap the blade laterally in the appropriate direction to straighten it. To retract the blade, tap the back of the plane body at roughly the same angle that the blade is bedded.

37 **Fine-tune blade placement.** Be mindful that once the wedge disengages the blade is free to drop out of the plane. I keep my thumb on the wedge with a bit of pressure as I back it out so that nothing comes loose and goes flying. Now that you know how to do this, you can make as many bench planes as you'd like. Different sizes, shapes, and bed angles to tackle any roughing, smoothing, or trimming tasks you may have.

CHAPTER 3

DOVETAILED BOX

We are humans. Humans have stuff. Some humans have a lot of stuff. Boxes are a great option for storing stuff. While there is no lack of options for boxes out there, in my opinion, none are as good and as attractive as handmade, wooden boxes.

This is the first project that features traditional dovetails, but please don't panic. They are like any other skill in woodworking—you simply learn how, then practice to get better at it. The nice thing about these boxes is that your first ones can get used in the shop and as you get better, you can feature them in your home. My first set of dovetails looked like they were chewed out by a famished beaver, so please don't worry about yours. If a set of dovetails you cut on your first boxes have gaps, simply fill them with wood filler and paint them. If you make one of these boxes a month, you will be cutting gap-free dovetails in no time.

The material I chose is white ash, but you can use any timber that you like. I like pine for many types of projects but in this case I would recommend staying away from it. Pine is soft and can deform easily, so I recommend waiting until your dovetailing game is up before trying softwoods. Poplar, cherry, or walnut are good woods to start with, to name a few. You can easily make this box your own by sizing components to suit your own stuff.

TOOLS

- Jack plane
- Smoothing plane
- Block planes
- Rip and crosscut saws
- Chisels
- Mallet
- Marking gauge
- Marking knife
- Dividers
- Chisels
- Mallet
- Dovetail saddle marker
- Dovetail saw
- Coping saw
- Rabbet plane
- Blue painter's tape
- Violin knife

MATERIALS

- PVA glue
- Small finish nails
- Wood wax

CUT LIST

PART	QTY	MATERIAL	LENGTH	WIDTH	THICKNESS
Long side	2	Solid	8"	2"	5/8"
Short side	2	Solid	6"	2"	5/8"
Top	1	Solid	8-1/16"	6-1/16"	5/8"
Bottom	1	Plywood	8-1/16"	6-1/16"	1mm

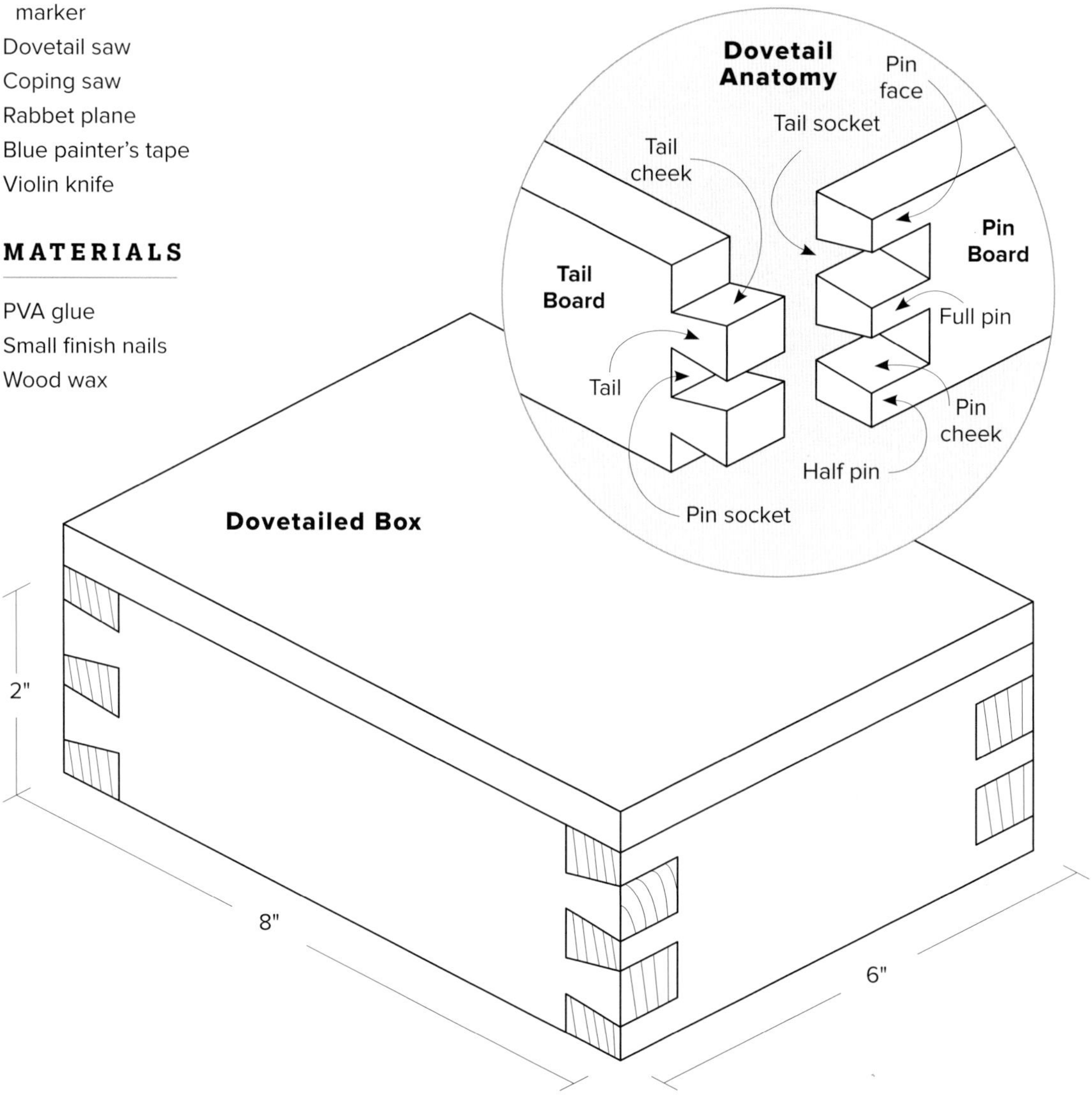

LAY OUT YOUR PARTS

1 Choose your materials. Start by cutting the box sides according to the cut list. Once you have the material dimensioned, lay out the pieces and choose which surfaces will be on the outside of your box. Generally, I position any "defects" on the inside of the box. That said, if the defect is nice looking, like a bark inclusion or sap line, then I might put it out for the world to see. Once you have picked the surfaces, lay the box out on your bench and mark the pieces with cabinetmaker's triangles to help keep track of their orientation. Because each dovetail joint will be hand-cut, each will only fit its mate. So don't lose track of the orientation or you'll get confused when it comes time for assembly.

2 Mark the ends for joinery. Set a marking gauge to the thickness of the box sides. This dimension will become the baseline for your dovetails. The longer box sides will become the tail boards while the shorter sides become the pin boards. Using the marking gauge, strike a line on the surfaces and edges of the tail boards and on only the faces on the pin boards. Don't panic if you strike a line where you weren't meant to—a few passes with a plane will get rid of them. You can put the pin boards aside for now and focus on the tail boards.

MARK OUT THE TAILS *(continued)*

3 Start with the tails. To begin laying out the tails, start by locating the half-pins ¼" from the edge of the board with a pencil. Do this on the ends of both tailboards.

4 Find the centerpoint. Use a set of dividers to locate the center of the board and make a light mark. Then mark the space between the two tails. Keep in mind that you must not make a space between the tails that is smaller than your smallest chisel. For example, if your smallest chisel is ¼", don't lay out a space of only ⅛" because you won't be able to easily clean out the waste. That being said, also don't go for a spacing of only ⅛" if this is your first crack at dovetails. Remember, you have to walk before running.

5 Size dovetails to you tools. Use your chisel to lay out this space by laying it down centered on the mark, then making a mark on either side of the chisel.

6 Mark tails on the faces. A handy tool to mark the tails is a dovetail saddle marker. This tool allows you to mark the angle and the straight line at the same time.

CUT THE TAILS

7 If it looks right, it is right. Set your dovetail marker on the end of the stock and pencil in the layout of the tails.

But don't start cutting into your box sides just yet! Take a moment to lay out some lines on a scrap of material and make a few practice cuts. I've cut a lot of dovetails over the years and I never skip the practice step. This activates your muscle memory and will warm you up to the task. It also reminds you to stand comfortably and get the first few cuts out of the way before moving to your box parts.

8 Make the first cuts. With the warm-up out of the way, saw on the lines, stopping before or at the baseline. In a later step you'll cut on a specific side of a mark, but for now splitting the line is fine. Make all of the cuts on each end. I like to rotate my workpiece to make the sloped lines vertical. Doing this allows me to saw straight up and down. Another method is to tilt the saw to match the lines. Either way works, you just have to choose which method works best for you.

CUT THE TAILS *(continued)*

9 | Cut the shoulders. Flip your pieces 90° and saw off the shoulder waste. In this case, be sure to cut on the waste side of the line. On a box, the first thing a person will see from the top is the shoulder, so a gap here is not ideal. Just be sure that you are on the waste side of the line with your saw and you'll be fine. No need to saw too far from the line, either. Be brave and save yourself all the extra work of paring to that line with chisels.

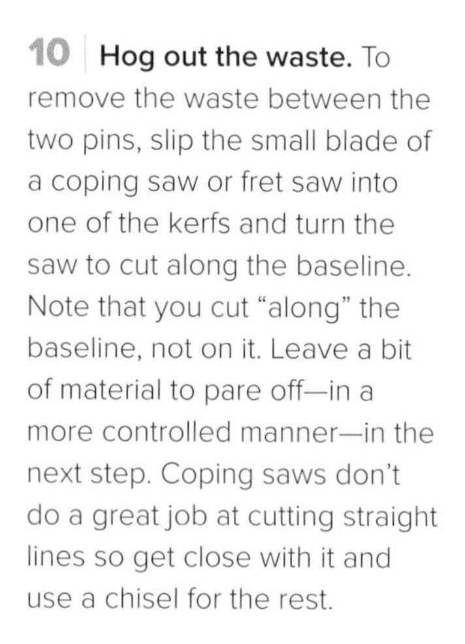

10 | Hog out the waste. To remove the waste between the two pins, slip the small blade of a coping saw or fret saw into one of the kerfs and turn the saw to cut along the baseline. Note that you cut "along" the baseline, not on it. Leave a bit of material to pare off—in a more controlled manner—in the next step. Coping saws don't do a great job at cutting straight lines so get close with it and use a chisel for the rest.

11 Square up the baseline. Use a chisel to remove the waste gradually. Keep in mind, you are only going to work about halfway through the board then you will repeat the process from the other side. If you try to go all the way though, there is no guarantee where you will come out at the bottom. Slowly work your way back to the baseline until you have just shy of 1⁄32" left, then place your chisel into the knife line you created at the start and pare the last of the waste away.

12 Slow and steady work. Keep everything square by holding your chisel straight up and down and lightly tapping the hammer to finish off the paring. Your eye alone is good judge of plumb lines, so trust what you see.

CUT THE TAILS *(continued)*

13 & 14 | Clean up the corners. Slide a wide chisel along the saw cuts and into the corners. It's critical that the corners be nice and clean so that the joint comes together well. For the space between the tails, you can use a chisel or a thin knife to get into the corners.

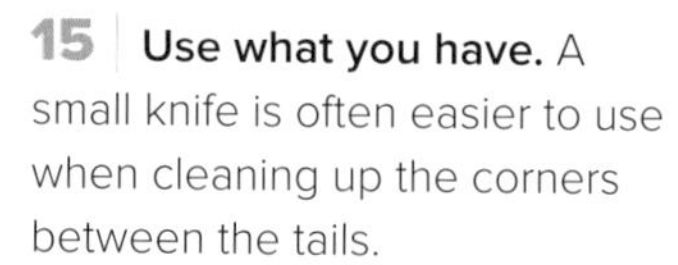

15 | Use what you have. A small knife is often easier to use when cleaning up the corners between the tails.

16 | Double-check your work. You want this as clean as possible for the next step—take the time to clean up as necessary. Once the tails on both ends of each long side are done, you can turn your attention to the pin boards.

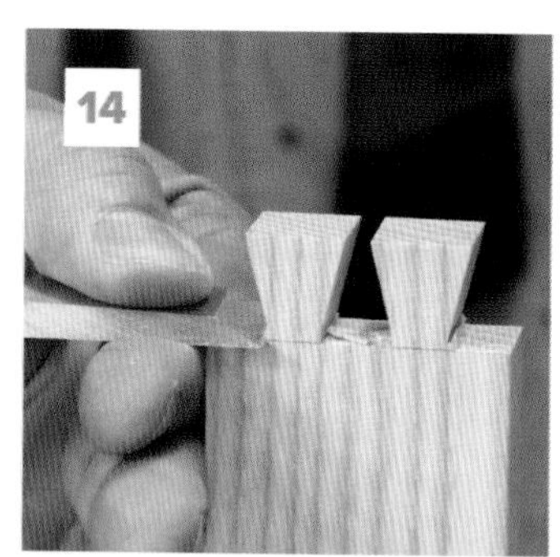

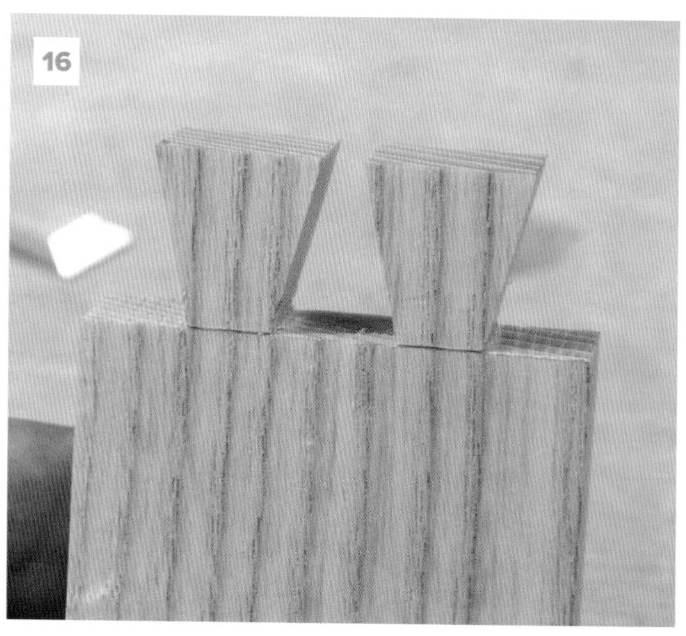

MARK & CUT THE PINS

17 | **Tape up the ends.** The first thing to do is put blue painter's tape on the ends of both pin boards. If you don't know why you're doing this, don't worry, you will see why soon enough. Be sure to trim the tape so there are no bits overhanging the edges.

18 | **Position the workpieces.** Take a moment here to reorient your parts. You will be using the tails that you just cut as a template to cut the pins, so it's essential to transfer the correct set of tails. Place the first pin board in the vise and use a block plane to help support the tail board so that the tails are flush to the pin board and the tail board is perpendicular to the pin board.

19 | **Cut around the tails.** Visually line up the tail board so that it's straight on the pin board and hold it down firmly with your hand. Use a marking knife to trace the sides of the tails, cutting through the tape.

MARK & CUT THE PINS *(continued)*

20 **Finish the layout.** Remove the blue tape on the section of the pin board that you need to remove. Then carry the knifed lines down the faces of the board using a square. Stop at the baselines.

21 **Saw to the baseline.** Pick up your back saw and begin sawing. Using the tape helps to ensure that you don't cut into the parts you want to save. If you remember to not cut the tape, you can't go wrong. With a bit of sensitivity, you should be able to feel the edge of the tape with your saw teeth. Once you place your saw, all that is left is to saw straight down to your baselines.

20

21

22 | Remove the bulk of the waste. Like with the tails, use the coping saw to remove the bulk of the waste piece by sawing along (not on) the baseline.

23 & 24 | Clean up the baseline. Then use a chisel to work your way back to the baseline as you did with the tails. You will have to angle your chisel left or right to prevent from cutting into the sides of the pins.

25 | Haste misses waste. Take the time to clean up the bottom of the pin sockets, ensuring that they are flat and the corners are free from all those crumbly bits.

TEST & FINE-TUNE THE FIT

26 | Make your life easy. Once all of your pins are looking good, you can start fitting the joints together. The first step is to use a knife or chisel to remove the inside corner of all the tails, creating a small chamfer. These chamfers won't be seen, but will allow you to ease the tails into the pins and reduce the risk of splinters coming off.

27 | Test your progress. Rub some soft pencil graphite just above where you chamfered the tails. This will help point out trouble spots as you test fit the joints.

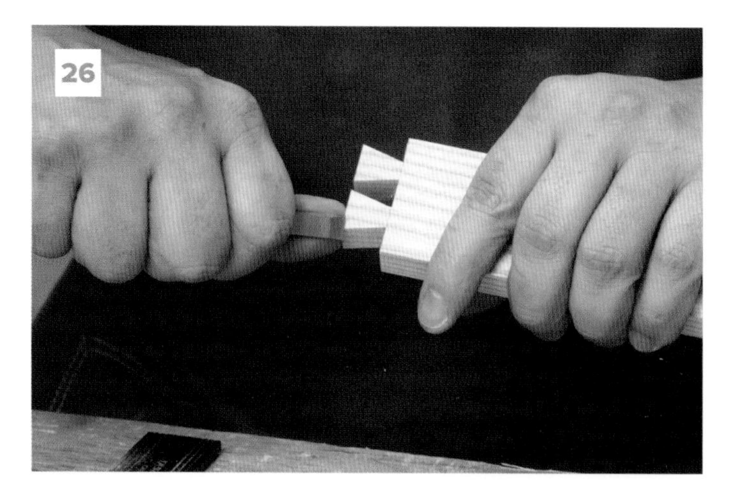
26

27

28

29

28 Check for the tight spots. The pencil marks will transfer graphite onto tight spots on the pins. That being said, do not remove any material from the tails. The tails were your pattern and if you start trimming them you will chase your own tail trying to make them fit.

29 Aim for a smooth fit. Use a sharp chisel to remove a tiny shaving of wood from the pins that have pencil on them and ensure that the sides of the pins remain plum. Repeat the paring step if necessary to get the tails to fit. The tails should require gentle persuasion with light hammer taps to send them home.

GLUE IT UP

30 | Prepare for assembly. The first step to any glue-up is to tidy up the area you are working on and lay down a piece of newsprint to keep the glue off of your bench.

There is an order to follow when gluing up dovetails to create a box. Start with one of the tail boards and one of the pin boards. Lay glue onto only the sides of the pins. There is no need to put glue at the bottom of the joint. Gluing this end-grain surface doesn't offer much glue strength.

31 | Bring it all together. Next, add the pin board to the other side of the tail board you started with so that you have one tail board and two pin boards glued together. The last piece to add is the second tail board by adding glue to the two sets of pins and installing the tail board. Throughout this process, use gentle taps with a mallet to bring the joints together and be sure to have a piece of sacrificial wood (something soft like pine) between the hammer and your box. This will protect your box pieces from damage and will spread the force out a bit.

32 **Look ma, no clamps.** The joints shouldn't require clamps to hold them together unless your joints are a bit loose. Once the pieces have come together, use a small square to ensure that the box is square. If it isn't, gently apply force with your hands to corners that are diagonal from each other to bring it into square.

33 **Clean up the joint.** Once the glue dries, you can start to level out the joints with a block plane. Because of the way we marked the baseline, there should be a bit of end grain to remove. Set the plane to take fine shavings and be sure to work from the outside of the box in to prevent spelching (blowing out end grain).

PREPARE THE TOP & BOTTOM

34 **Clean up the edges.** Now turn your attention to the top and bottom of the box. Using the block plane again, level off the edges so that they are flush. Also make sure that these surfaces are flat and don't rock when you place them on a flat surface. If the assembly does rock, remove material from the high corners until it sits well.

35 **Cut out the bottom.** This is a small box, so the bottom is simply a small piece of Baltic birch plywood nailed into place. To limit tear-out while sawing, start by applying blue tape on the approximate area of the plywood where you are going to cut. Now trace the box on the plywood and saw just outside of the lines to ensure that the ply is a bit oversized. I own a Japanese saw ground specifically for clean cuts in sheet stock, but any fine-tooth crosscut saw should do the trick.

PREPARE THE TOP & BOTTOM *(continued)*

36 | Attach the bottom. Use some small finish nails to tack the bottom into place. You can glue the bottom on but that will make it more difficult to replace the bottom if the need arises.

37 | Ease the edges. With the bottom installed, use a block plane to trim it flush to the box sides and apply a shallow chamfer on it. This chamfer will make it so you can't see the plywood on the bottom—all you will see is a thin shadow line.

38 | Prepare the top. Break out the material for the lid of the box cutting it a bit oversized (1⁄16" larger in each dimension) and plane to final thickness. Place the lid onto the box and as shown and mark where the inside of the box contacts the lid. These marks will locate the rabbets cut along the edges of the box top.

PREPARE THE TOP & BOTTOM *(continued)*

39 | Rabbet the long-grain sides. Set up a rabbet plane to cut the rabbets you marked out on both of the long-grain sides.

40 | Adjust for the ends. Once the side rabbets are cut, lower the nicker to cut the cross-grain rabbets on the ends of the top. The leading nicker scores the wood ahead of the blade, which helps prevent tear-out to create a crisp line as you cut.

41 | Create a perfect fit. Once the lid fits in place, use a smoothing plane to flush up the top with the long sides of the box. If you'd like, you can leave the short edges of the lid a bit oversized to act as a convenient way to lift off the lid. Simply slide your fingers up the side of the box and they will catch the lid.

42 Simple finishes are best. Boxes aren't usually subject to a lot of wear and tear (unless they are in your shop) so you can usually get away with a sheer finish. As a rule, I try to get away with the lightest finish I can because I've never been a big fan of the candy-coated look. A light coat of wood wax on this project is plenty of protection, and you can always add more wax as time goes on.

Now that you know how to make boxes and cut dovetails you will find all sorts of stuff to put in them. You can make them custom-sized for all sorts of things around the house and in the shop. They make great gifts and your skills will increase with every one you make.

CHAPTER 4

PERCH STOOL

Some woodworkers prefer to stand when they are at the bench, while others prefer to sit. I like to do a bit of both, and often find myself in a perched position. When I looked at redesigning my trusty bench stool, I realized that I always seem to sit right at the edge so that I can easily lean forward. That got me thinking—maybe I need a way to lean forward while still keeping myself planted on the seat . . . like a rocker on a rocking chair! That, combined with some inspiration from the Conoid chair by George Nakashima, led to this minimalist and highly functional design. I was also inspired by some simple stools that I have seen in Mark Harrell's shop (maker and owner of Bad Axe Tool Works). Mark's were made from 2-by stock and plywood, but the design hints were there for me to utilize.

When you make this perch, you can decide whether or not you want the tilt feature, but I think the ability to lean forward as you work is pretty cool. I made most of my perch with black cherry, but the legs are hard maple with a hint of bird's-eye figure. Ultimately you can make the perch out of whatever you like, but I would stick to a hardwood for strength and durability.

TOOLS

- Jack plane
- Smoothing plane
- Rip and crosscut saws
- Drilling jig
- Cordless drill
- ⅜" Forstner bit
- Chisels
- Mallet
- Marking gauge
- Marking knife
- Rasp
- Bow saw or coping saw
- #8 pilot/countersink drill bit
- Nicholson Super Shear file (optional)
- Curved spokeshave (optional)
- Chairmaker's pencil gauge (optional)

CUT LIST

PART	QTY	LENGTH	WIDTH	THICKNESS
Seat	1	17"	8"	1"
Leg	2	25-½"	2-½"	¾"
Foot	2	16"	3-⅜"	1"
Footrest	1	12-¾"	3-¼"	¾"
Seat stretcher	1	12-¾"	2"	¾"
#8 screws	3	1-¼"		

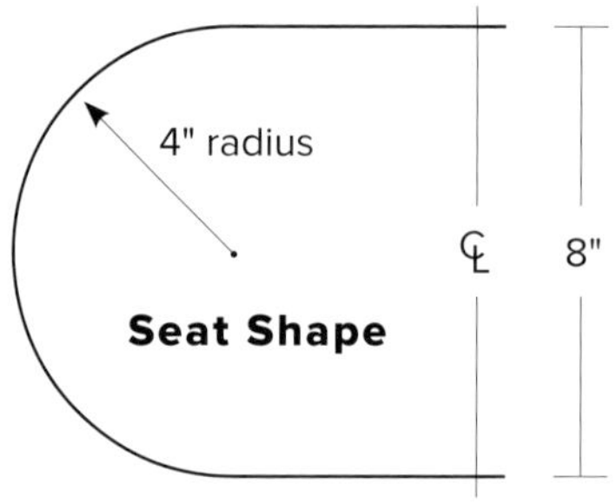

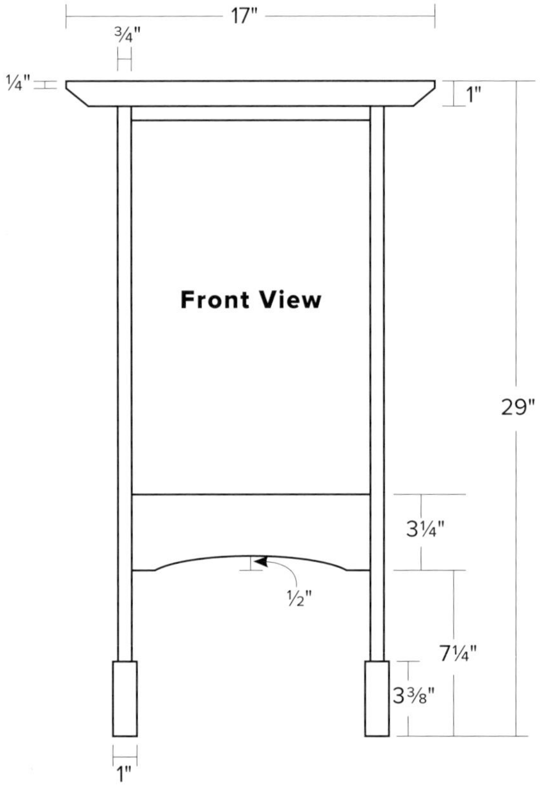

17"
¾"
¼"
1"
Front View
29"
3¼"
½"
7¼"
3⅜"
1"

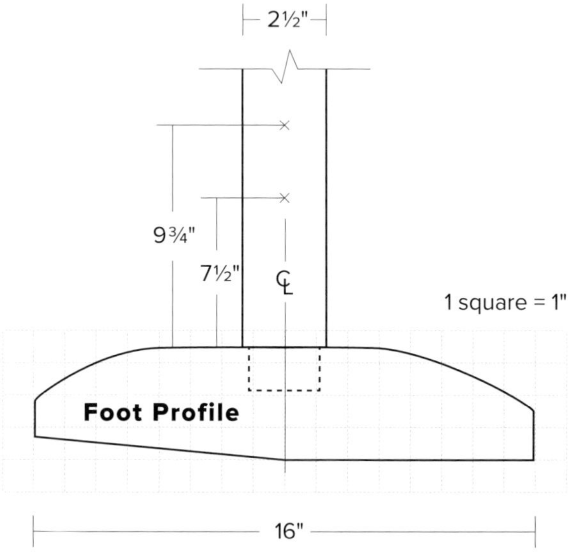

4" radius
℄
8"
Seat Shape

2½"
9¾"
7½"
℄
1 square = 1"
Foot Profile
16"

PLAN OUT THE PARTS

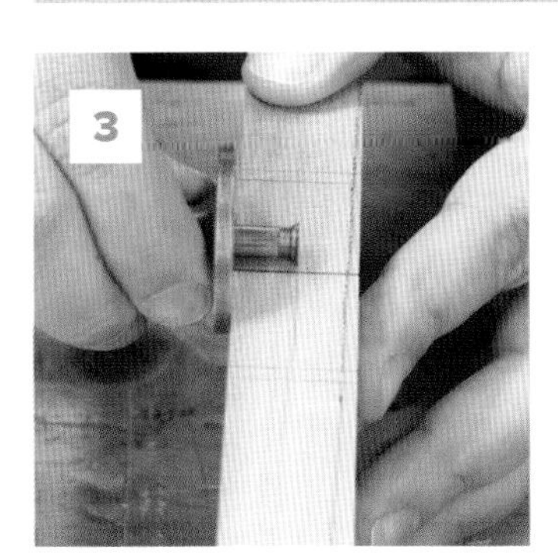

1 Choose your materials. Start by laying out all of your components on to the rough boards. Breakout the stock and dress the lumber to final dimensions.

2 Plan for joinery early. Before you do any shaping to the feet, lay out the mortises that will receive the tenons on the bottoms of the legs. Clamp the two foot pieces together then find the centerline on the length and width of the legs and mark where the legs will be on the feet.

3 Work from a centerline. Locate the center of the mortise with a marking gauge

4 Mark the mortise width. Reset the marking gauge to mark a line 3⁄16" away from the center on both sides. This creates the outline for a 3⁄8" mortise.

MORTISE FOR THE LEGS

5 Prepare your mortising tools. If you have access to a drill press, you can use that to start drilling out the waste of the mortise, making a series of holes along the length of the mortise. Alternatively, you can use a drilling jig modified with a couple of fences to center it. Nothing too fancy here, just a couple of straight and square scraps and a few C-clamps to hold them in place. Use a bushing on the drill bit to limit the depth of the mortises according to the drawing.

6 Position the jig. Place the drilling jig on the edge of the board.

7 Drill out the ends. For this task, it will be best if you use a ⅜" Forstner bit so you can overlap the holes. Begin by drilling holes at both ends of the mortise. Doing this establishes the final width of the mortise and ensures that the mortise ends are clean and crisp.

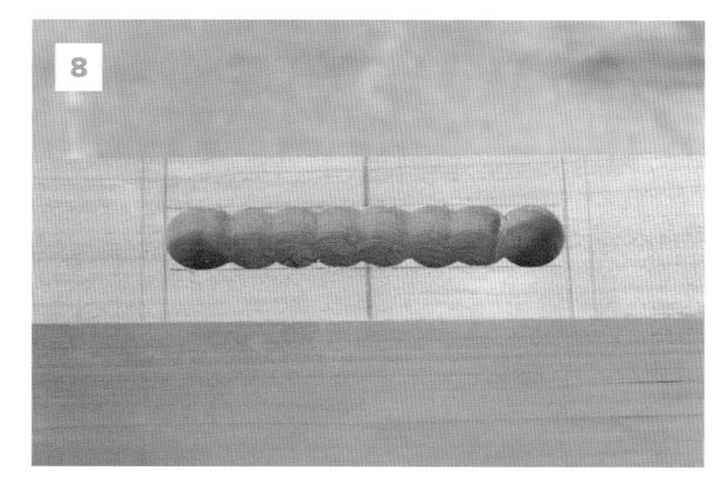

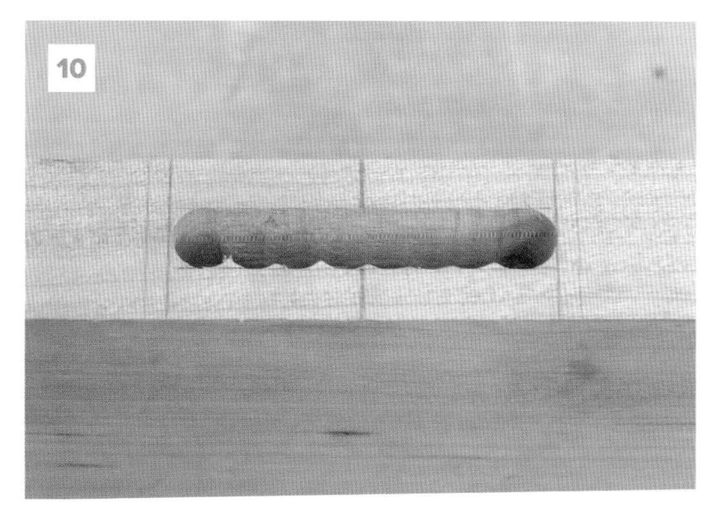

8 Hog out the waste. Drill a series of holes that slightly overlap to create the rough mortise. This will make cleaning out the waste easier and quicker.

9 Trim to the line. Once the waste is drilled out, use your widest chisel that will fit between the two ends of the mortise to pare out the remaining waste. Simply put the chisel into the knife line you created and push the chisel straight down.

10 Leave a clean cheek. Make a smooth cut down both sides of the mortise and leave the ends rounded. It is much easier to round tenons than it is to square mortises cut this way.

MARK OUT THE TENONS

11 | Set your marking gauge. Now you can move on to the second part of the joint—the tenon. Use a marking gauge to find the true depth of the mortise then back off the setting about 1⁄16". Doing this will guarantee that the tenon will not end up too long, which would prevent the joint from coming together.

12 | Mark the tenon shoulder. Mark a line all the way around the bottom of the legs to set the shoulder of the tenon.

13 | Mark the tenon width. Lay the leg down in line with the foot, center it on the mortise, and make a small mark on the leg material to locate the cheeks. Reset the marking gauge to mark out the 3⁄8" tenon.

CUT THE TENONS

14 | Finish up the layout. Mark the short shoulders according to the drawing on p. 58, then you are ready to saw the tenon to width.

15 | Create a quick jig. Start making the tenon by making the crosscuts. In this case I made a simple sawing jig that helps with sawing straight. Think of this jig as a set of training wheels for a bicycle. You won't need it forever, but it helps to teach you what sawing straight feels like as you develop your muscle memory. The jig is made from a square piece of stock with a few magnets mounted flush to the surface. These magnets hold the saw straight as you cut.

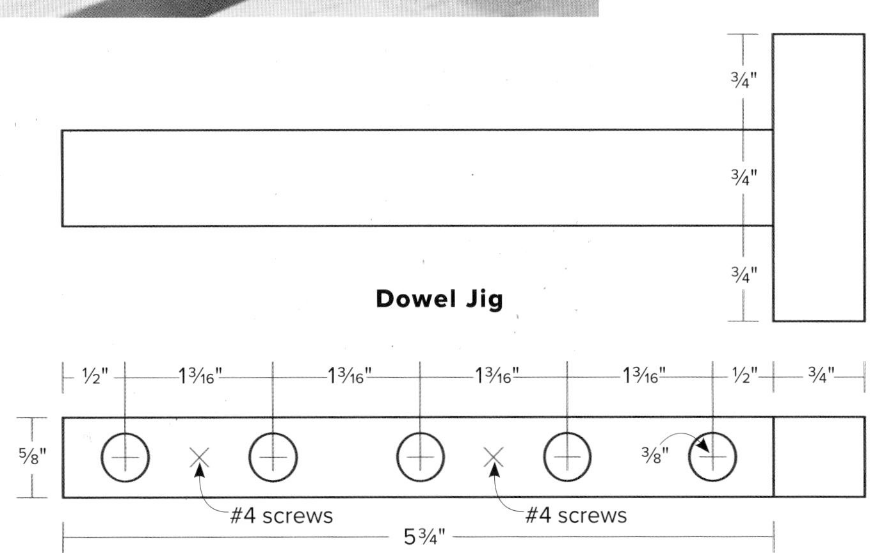

CUT THE TENONS *(continued)*

16 | **Cut the shoulder.** Begin with the jig aligned along the mark created by the marking gauge.

17 & 18 | **Saw the cheeks.** Hold the leg at an angle and saw diagonally on one corner, then tilt the leg the other way and saw on the opposite corner. The cuts should line up (more or less) in the center.

19 | **Connect the cuts.** Then hold the leg vertically and saw straight down until you are just above the shoulder line. This technique helps to keep the cuts straight by helping the saw track well. Finish off by sawing the narrow shoulder off, being sure to stop at the shoulder line. Use a chisel to straighten out any of your cuts and clean up the corners where the cheeks meet the shoulders.

ROUND OVER THE TENONS

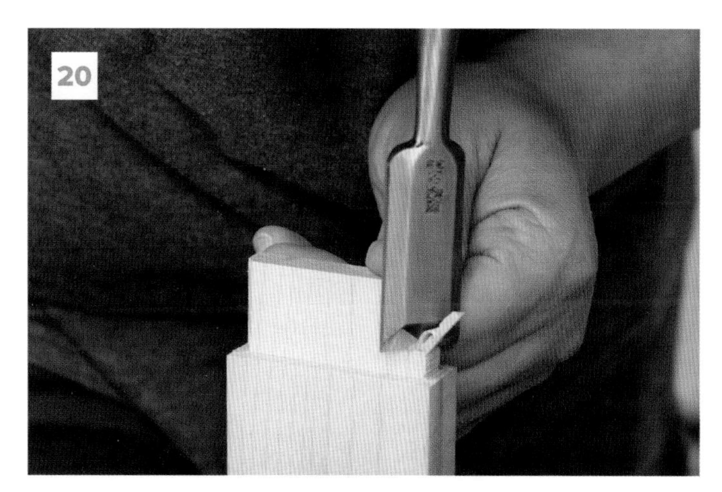

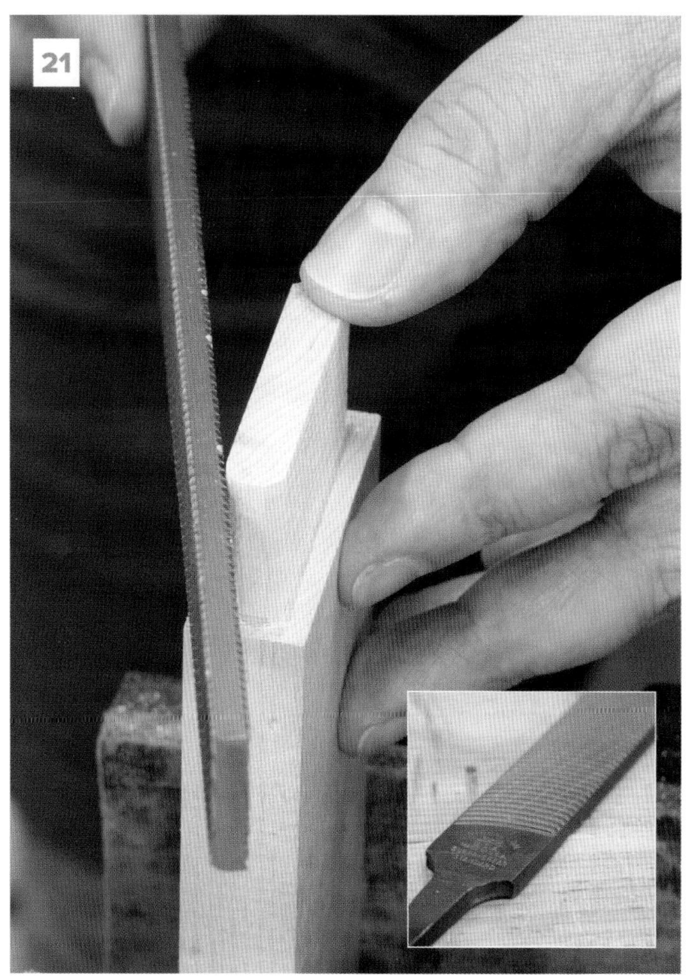

20 Round the tenon ends. Start by using a chisel to remove the corners of the tenons.

21 File it away. Then use the file to round the corners. My favorite file for this job is a Nicholson Super Shear. This file is extremely sharp and has safe edges that won't cut into the shoulder as you work.

ROUND OVER THE TENONS *(continued)*

22 | Refine the tenons. Don't panic if they aren't perfect, you can make adjustments as you go. Test-fit the joint to make sure they fit well.

23 | Aim for a smooth fit. You should be able to assemble the joint with hand pressure. There should be sufficient friction in the joint to keep the pieces together.

CREATE A DOWEL JOINT

24

25

26

24 Locate the footrest on the leg. Now you can move on to a different type of joinery. The footrest for the perch is attached using dowels. Start by locating the footrest on the leg according to the drawing, then use a marking gauge to find the center of the width of the leg.

25 Position the dowel on the leg. Now lay out the hole locations for the dowels on the leg and on the footrest. Then use an awl to pierce the surface of the wood.

26 Mark the mating foot-rest. Finish the layout by striking a line locating the center of the thickness of the footrest.

CREATE A DOWEL JOINT *(continued)*

27 | **Drill the first dowel hole.** Using a drill press or drilling jig, set the bit depth so that you don't blow out the side of the leg then drill the holes for the dowels.

28 | **Drill the mating piece.** Then reset the stop bushing to give you a 1"-deep hole and drill the holes into the end grain of the footrest.

29 | **The holes align.** The result is a set of corresponding holes that will locate the footrest and hold it firmly in place.

CUT THE DOVETAIL

30

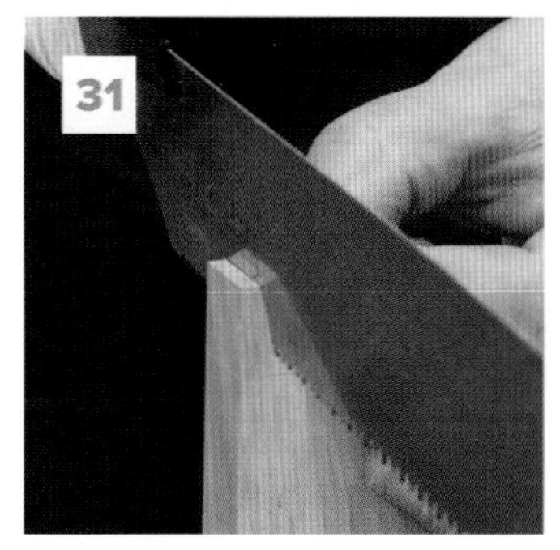

31

32

33

30 Move to the dovetails. The final bit of joinery is dovetails for the seat stretcher. This component will help stiffen up the perch and will provide a convenient way to fasten the seat. Lay out a dovetail on both ends of the stretcher according to the drawing.

31 Guide the cut. Set the teeth of the blade in the groove created by your marking gauge. Then angle the blade to match the angle of the dovetail, and use your index finger to guide the cut.

32 Cut the shoulder. Clamp the stretcher horizontally in your vise and cut the shoulder. Clean up the cuts using a chisel.

33 Mark out the pins. Transfer the tail to the top of the legs. I apply blue tape to the top of the pin board, then use spacer stock to locate the tail board flush to the pin board. Note that the stretcher is narrower than the legs, so ensure the tails are centered on the legs. Marking the pins with a marking knife in the blue tape makes it easy to see the correct position.

CUT THE DOVETAIL *(continued)*

34 | Clean up the joint. Remove the waste of the pin area using a chisel and mallet. To prevent blowing out the narrower face of the pin board, cut with the narrow face up on your bench.

35 | Test the fit. Aim for a joint that goes together with hand pressure and closes up with, at most, a few taps of your mallet.

CREATE TWO MATCHING FEET

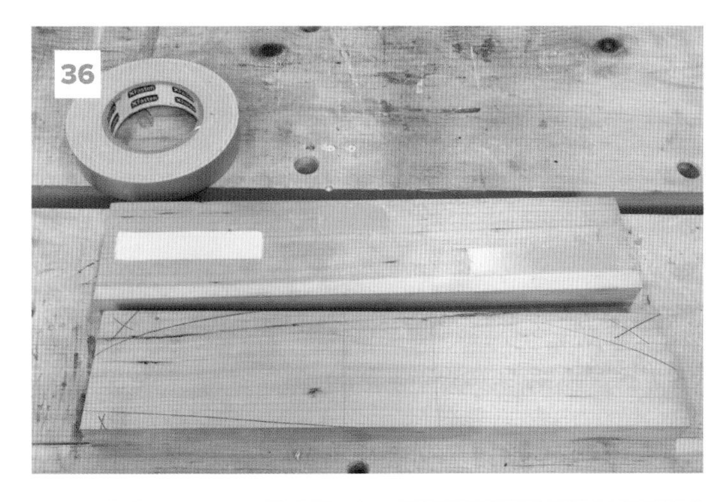

36 | Draw the foot profile. Start by orienting the two feet correctly. Lay out the foot shape and rocker taper on one surface. Then join the feet together using double-sided tape. It's best to lay out and cut the components together whenever you can.

37 | Cut them to shape. Use a panel saw to cut the straight line that forms the rocker at the bottom of the foot. Stay on the waste side of the line as you cut.

38 | Smooth it out. With both feet still taped together, use a handplane to true up your cut.

CREATE TWO MATCHING FEET *(continued)*

39 | **Survey your work.** Ensure that the new edges you've created are square and true.

40 | **Saw it to shape** Use a bow saw to cut the curves on the tops of the feet. Again, leave the pencil line so you have some room to true up your cuts.

41 | **Refine the curve.** Use a block plane to refine the curves on the top edges of the feet.

42 **The feet are separate but equal.** Once you have faired the curve, pull the two feet apart to reveal two matching profiles. Use a block plane to create chamfers on the edges of both feet, relieving all of the arrises.

43 **Clean up the edges.** The key to getting chamfers of consistent size by hand is to count the number of strokes it takes to get a pleasing chamfer. Then take the same number of strokes for all chamfers all around.

CUT AN ARCH IN THE FOOTREST

44 | **Shape the footrest.** Start by laying out reference marks near the ends of the footrest using a square to match the profile of the drawing on p. 58.

45 | **Draw in a curve.** Connect the marks using a drawing bow or wooden batten. You can buy a bow or you can make one easily enough with some string and a strip of tempered Masonite.

46 | **Cut and clean the curve.** Cut close to (but leave) the line with a bow saw. Then clean up the cut using a curved spokeshave—a tool perfectly suited to working concave curves. If you don't have a spokeshave, clean up the cut using sandpaper wrapped around a thin, flexible scrap of wood.

SHAPE THE SEAT

47 **Mark out the ends.** The final bit of shaping happens on the seat. This will require forming a chamfer on a curve, which can take a bit of practice. Remember, you can always practice skills on a piece of scrap wood before applying them to your project material. Lay out the two half-circles on both ends of the seat using a compass.

48 **Cut it out.** Saw away the waste with a bowsaw, leaving the pencil line. Then clean up the cut using a block plane.

49 **A chamfer refines the look.** Lay out the chamfer on the edges and start shaping using a plane, working on the long edges first. I'm using a chairmaker's pencil gauge, but a combination square and pencil will work as well.

SHAPE THE SEAT *(continued)*

50 **Relieve the edge.** Use a plane to create a chamfer on the lower, outer edge of the seat. Use your eye to gauge the chamfer you are making so that it stays centered between the two layout lines.

51 **Chamfer the ends.** Then do the same thing with the two curved ends of the seat.

52 **Soften hard edges.** Finish off the seat by easing the corners of the top to make it more comfortable to sit on.

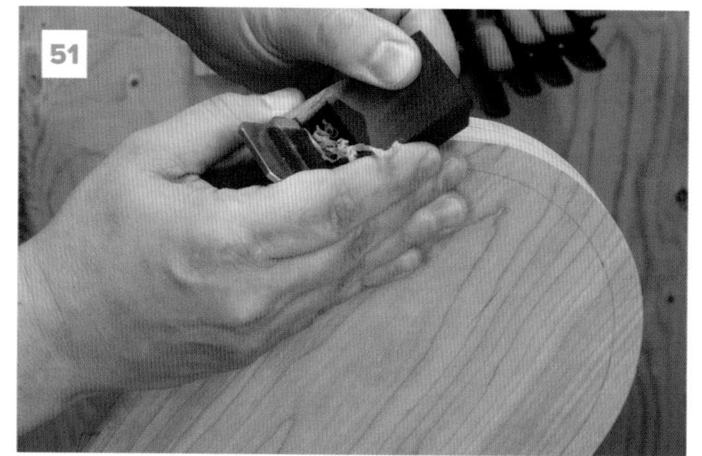

ASSEMBLE THE PERCH

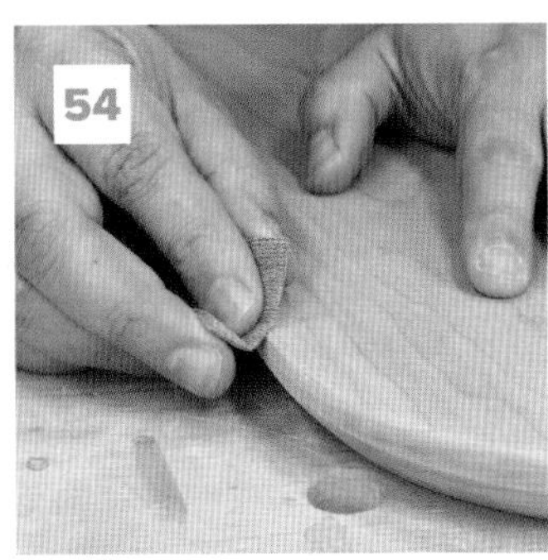

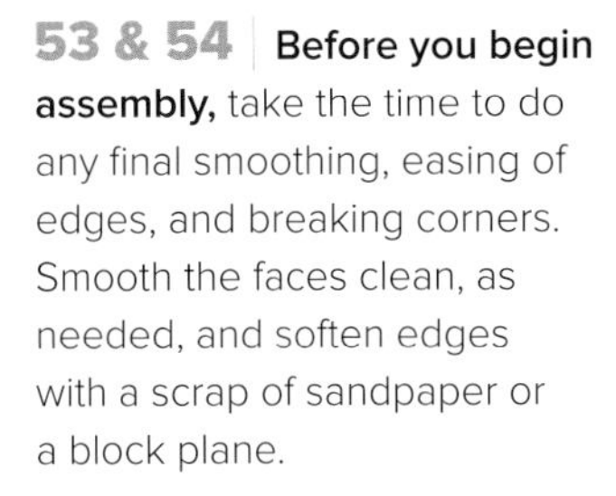

53 & 54 | Before you begin assembly, take the time to do any final smoothing, easing of edges, and breaking corners. Smooth the faces clean, as needed, and soften edges with a scrap of sandpaper or a block plane.

55 | Drill for the seat. The seat attaches to the stretcher from underneath. Drill three pilot holes and countersinks into the seat stretcher.

56 | Break out the glue. The first step of the assembly is to glue the feet to the legs. Place some glue in the top half of the mortise then slide the tenon in until it goes in all the way.

ASSEMBLE THE PERCH *(continued)*

57 Clamp up the legs and feet. You only need to put glue on the top half of the mortise because it will get dragged through to the bottom. Don't use too much glue because you risk a hydraulic lock, which can lead to parts breaking. Use a clamp to hold things in place while the glue dries.

58 It's a standup job. Assemble the footrest using glue and dowels. Make sure the dowels aren't too long so they don't interfere with the fit. Once the parts are glued and fit together, place a clamp across the assembly to hold it in place.

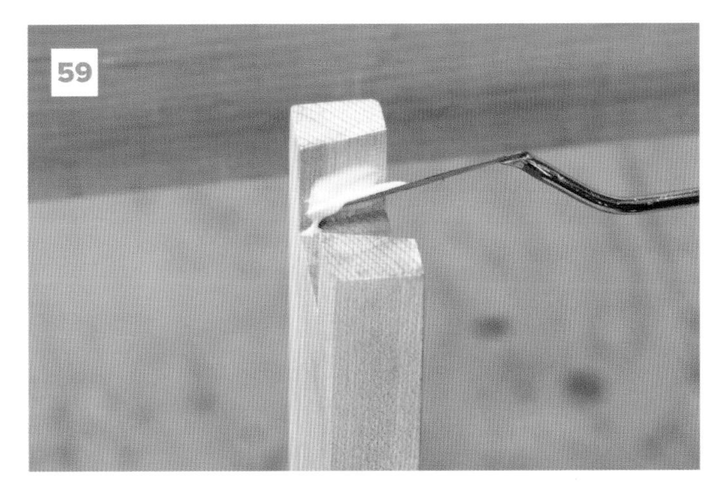

59 **Attach the seat.** Begin by applying glue between the pins on the end of the legs.

60 **Clamp it in place.** Slide the seat stretcher dovetail in place atop the legs and clamp it on either end. Once it sets up a bit, clean up any glue squeeze-out—the glue will have a rubbery consistency. Leave the assembly in the clamps for at least 2-3 hours before moving on to the final part of assembly.

ASSEMBLE THE PERCH *(continued)*

61 | **Bring it together.** Once the glue has set, place the seat top down on your bench and position the legs over it.

62 | **Drill into the seat.** Center **the** stretcher on the seat then place a drill bit into the hole to mark the location of the attachment holes. Then drill the pilot holes.

61

62

63 Fasten the seat in place. Complete the assembly by attaching the seat using #8 1-½"-long screws.

64 Lay on a finish. With the assembly done, all you have to do is apply your finish of choice. I chose to use Furniture Butter, which is a product made from natural oils and wax.

Though this perch is a bit unorthodox, I think you will find that using it at the bench for the type of close focus we do as woodworkers, will be beneficial. Being able to lean forward by rocking on the feet will save you from rounding your back and causing undue strain.

THE
TRAGICALLY
HIP

CHAPTER 5

ALBUM CRATE

Vinyl is making a resurgence lately, but storing it can be a challenge. In the old days, you could score a few milk crates and be done with it. Newer milk crates don't fit albums, however, so don't risk jail time stealing them. And fear not; you're a woodworker who can make your own.

The crates in this chapter are made from pine so that they patina nicely and are inexpensive to make. It's also easier to find wide boards in pine than it is in other species. Choose ¾"-thick 1x12 stock that is as straight as possible to reduce the amount of flattening you'll have to do. These crates are not just good for albums of course, you can use them for anything, really. I like them in the shop—they're a low-tech container that can hold things like clamps or power cords. You can even label them using card holders to make it easy to figure out what's in them. These crates even have a design feature that allows you to stack them if you want.

You may think that using a dovetail is a bit of overkill, and you're probably right. These dovetails are unconventional as the pins are cut into long grain as opposed to end grain. This makes the crate extremely strong. And, of course, using dovetails in this project is a great way to practice cutting them.

TOOLS

- Jack plane
- Smoothing plane
- Block planes
- Rip and crosscut saws
- Chisels
- Mallet
- Marking gauge
- Marking knife
- Chisels
- Mallet
- Dovetail saddle marker
- Dovetail saw
- Coping saw
- Rabbet plane
- Blue painter's tape
- Violin knife

CUT LIST

PART	LENGTH	WIDTH	THICKNESS
Sides	14-½"	9-¼"	¾"
Bottom	12-¾"	9-¼"	¾"
Wide slats	14-¼"	3-½"	¾"
Narrow slats	14-¼"	2"	¾"

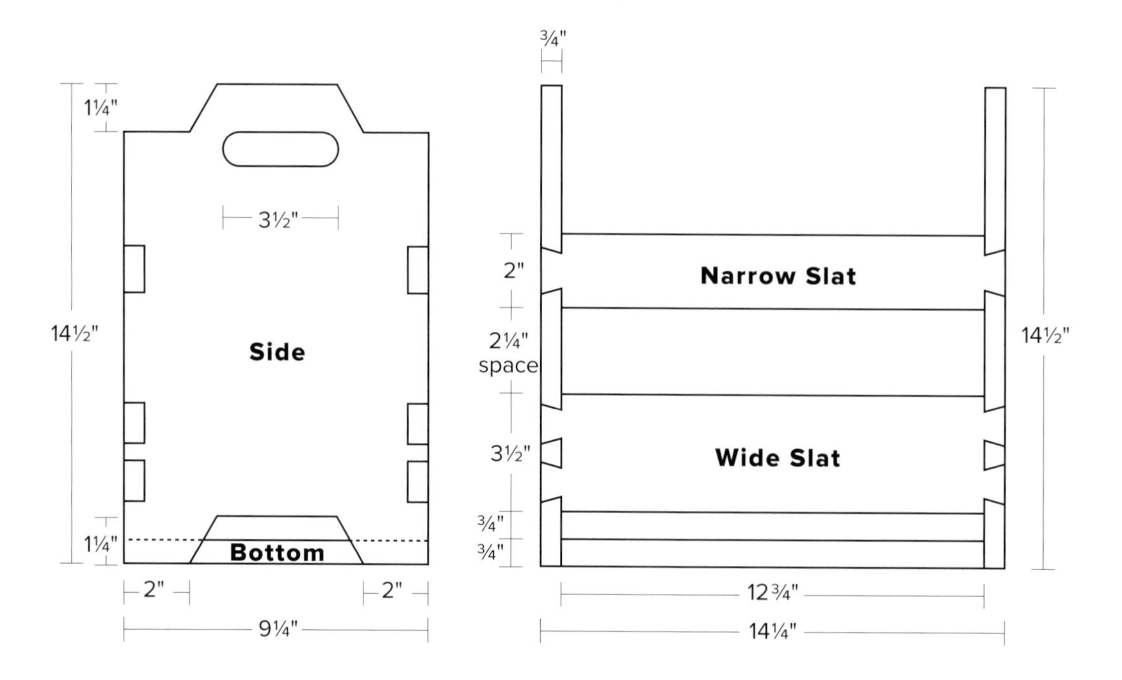

PREP THE STOCK

1 & 2 | Choose your stock. To begin, start by breaking out the lumber to the sizes you need for all the components. Keep in mind that if you are making multiple crates, you'll need to create more parts as necessary. Start with the crosscuts then move on to the rip cuts.

3 | Smooth the edges. Remove the rough-sawn edges using a handplane. If you built the new wooden plane earlier in this book, this is a great opportunity to use it.

PREP THE STOCK *(continued)*

4 | Clean up the faces. Finish off by smoothing the boards to get rid of any milling marks.

5 | Don't lose your place. Use a cabinetmaker's triangle to sort out your parts and consider using different colors of lead to mark your parts if you are making more than one crate.

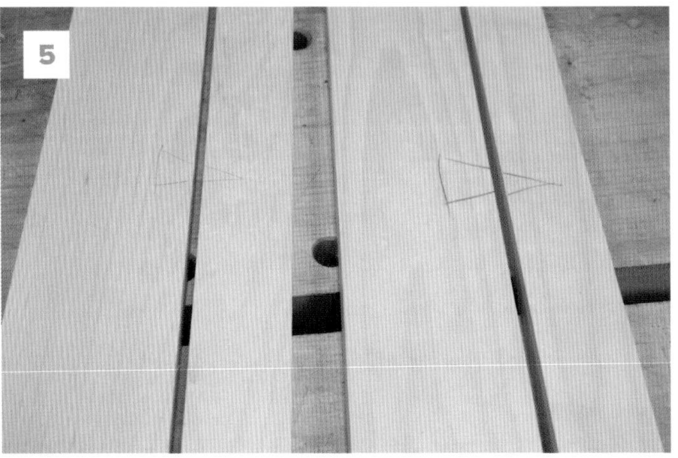

LAY OUT & CUT THE TAILS

6 | Mark the baselines. Set a marking gauge to the thickness of your components and mark the baselines on all of the slat pieces, then lay out the dovetails according to the drawing.

7 | Lay out the tails. Use the drawing on p. 84 as a guide for laying out the tails. If you need a reminder on how the layout of dovetails works, go back to Chapter 4 (p. 66) to refresh your memory. Then saw out the tails with a back saw.

8 | Use a handy guide. You'll notice that I'm using another tool in conjunction with the back saw, this a dovetail saw guide. Dovetail guides are fantastic tools to help you learn the angle you need to saw when cutting dovetails. Think of them as training wheels. They help hold the saw at the correct angle so that you can focus on other things, and they can be used with push or pull saws. Keep in mind that if you use Western saws, you will likely need a carcass saw to ensure that you have enough room under the saw's back.

LAY OUT & CUT THE TAILS *(continued)*

9 | Saw out the waste. Remove the material between the tails using a coping saw. Saw as close to the baseline as you're comfortable, but take care not to overcut.

10 | Clean up the baseline. Remove the remaining waste with a chisel. Aim for a flat surface across the thickness of the board—any protrusion will prevent the board from closing up.

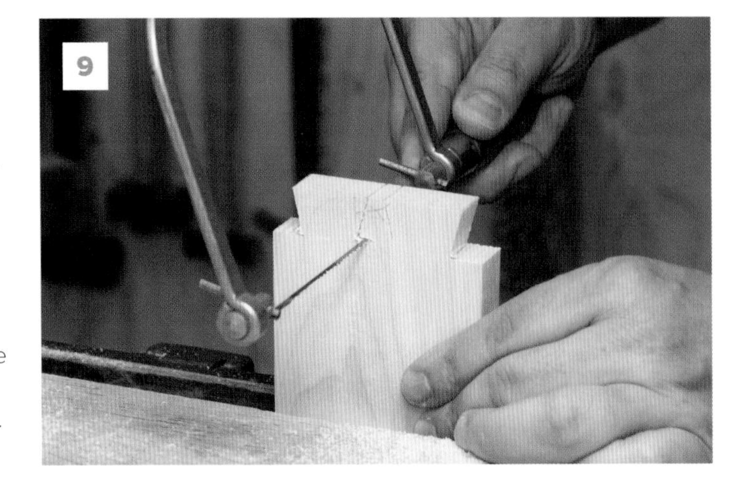

MARK OUT THE MATING JOINERY

11 | **Position the slats on the sides.** Once you have all the tails cut and cleaned up on the slats, reference the drawing on p. 84 to determine the location of the slats on the sides of the crate. Clamp the two sides together and mark them at the same time to eliminate the chance of error. This layout is a bit unconventional in that the pins are not being marked on the end grain surface of the board. This can make the pins more fragile, so be careful handling them.

12 | **Cut in the baselines.** Use a marking gauge set to the thickness of the slats to cut a line between the slat layout marks. There is no need to mark them along the whole surface because they are only needed at the slat locations.

13 | **Mark out the tails.** Position the slats according to your cabinetmaker's marks to make sure you have the correct slats in the correct orientation.

MARK OUT THE MATING JOINERY *(continued)*

14 | **Knife around the tails.** We are not using blue tape here so make a few passes with the knife to ensure well-established knife lines.

15 | **Give your eyes a break.** To help with seeing those lines, use a 0.3mm mechanical pencil to darken the knife lines. The small diameter of this graphite will drop into the knifed lines, making them easier to see.

16 | **Saw out the tails.** Marking the waste with an "X" helps remind you which side of the line to cut on. In the photos, I've switched to using a Japanese crosscut saw called a kataba. This saw has fine teeth and will leave a clean exit with little spelching. I'm still using the jig for these cuts so that they match exactly with tail cuts.

17 | **Remove the waste.** Once again, remove the bulk of the waste with the coping saw and chisel out the rest

18 | **Clean up the cuts.** When chiseling out the waste, be mindful that you are going across the long grain which requires far less force then cutting end grain, so use a gentle hand.

ASSEMBLE THE JOINTS

19 Test and adjust the fit. With all of the pins cut out and cleaned, begin fitting the slat joints. Remember to pare material only off of the pin board side of the joint when fitting things together; use light cuts and check the fit often.

20 Close up the joint. Light mallet taps are all you should need to get the tails to slide into place—anything more than that means the joints are too tight.

21 Gauge your progress. With all of the joinery cut, you finally can envision the finished crate.

19

20

21

22 **When good joints go bad.** As mentioned earlier, the pins here are more delicate than more typical dovetail joints, so be gentle. I am telling you this from experience. It seems no matter how long you've been woodworking, things can still not go according to plan. If you've had an incident like I did here, don't panic.

23 **A little glue to the rescue.** Simply glue the pin back on with some wood glue and hold it in place with some binding tape.

SHAPE THE SIDES

24 Lay out the side patterns. As a rule, it is always preferable to cut the joinery before shaping. This is because the pieces are generally flat and square prior to shaping. Now that the joinery is cut and fit, it's time to shape the sides. Take a look at the drawing and lay out the handle holes and shapes that will allow these crates to stack. I've used ink here which makes things easier to see. If you're curious, I use Sharpie "no bleed" pens that have a 0.5mm tip.

25 Work from the top down. Start at the top of the sides by cutting down to the horizontal layout line.

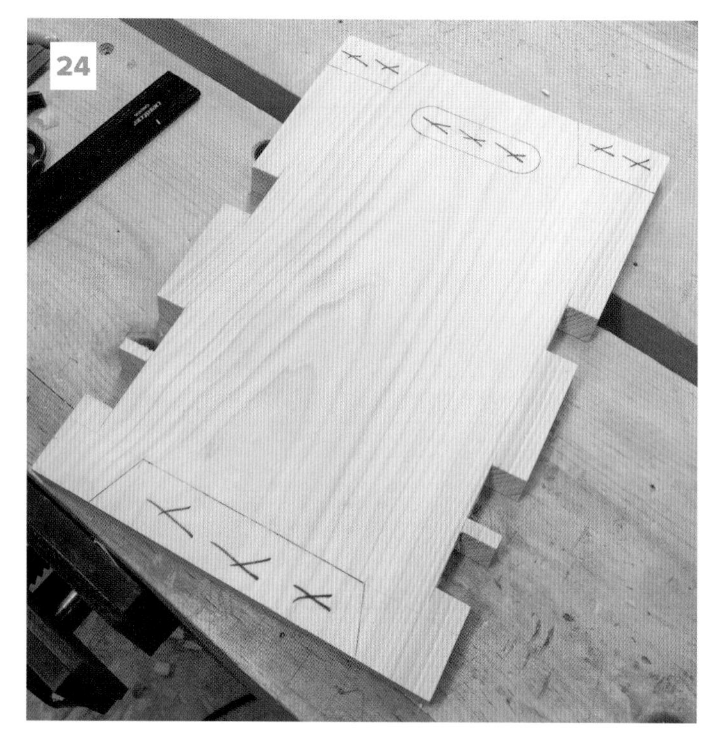

24

25

26 | Cut in from the edge. Turn the board 90° and crosscut on the line to meet the sloped kerf you just cut. I'm using a saw guide here to keep the cut as straight as possible but it's not necessary. Slow down as you approach the existing kerf so that you don't accidentally cut into the side.

27 | Saw out the waste. At the bottom of the side, cut the two sloped lines, stopping at the baseline, then grab your trusty coping saw to remove the bulk of the waste cutting just above the layout line.

28 | Clean up the edges. Make a simple paring jig by jointing a scrap of hardwood to create a square corner. I've added a strip of high-friction tape on the underside of my jig to prevent slipping. If you don't have any of this tape, then a bit of #150-grit sandpaper adhered to the bottom will do the trick. Clamp the paring jig onto the layout line firmly and use your widest chisel to pare the remaining waste. Nibble away at it slowly so that your chisel doesn't dive in. Using the hardwood scrap as a paring guide will allow you to work all the way through to the other side without the risk of a slanted cut.

CREATE THE HANDLE

29 | **Move on to the handle.** Start by drilling two holes at either end of the handle using a 1" bit, then remove the remaining waste in the center with a ⅞" bit, drilling holes close together.

30 | **Chisel away the waste.** Make sure that you put a piece of waste material under the workpiece so that the bit doesn't blow out the back side. Clamp the paring jig on the layout line and nibble away at the waste until you hit the line.

31 Smooth the transitions. Use a small rasp and/or file to smooth out any bumps between the holes drilled to create the handle.

32 Simple tools are best. Take the time now to refine all of your shapes and surfaces. You can use sandpaper and a variety of sanding blocks to get the job done. A dowel wrapped with sandpaper is a handy tool for cleaning up inside curves.

33 Take the edge off. Knocking off all the sharp corners prior to assembly makes your life a bit easier. Once everything is sanded to your satisfaction, you are ready to begin assembling the crate.

ASSEMBLE THE CRATE

34 Glue the sides in place. Attach the two slats on one side first, then do the same for the other side. For this project, you can put glue on the bottom of the joint because there is long grain at the base. You'll notice this is different than in the chapter about the dovetailed box, where I talked about not putting glue on the bottom. It all depends on what you are making.

35 Install the bottom. Once the glue has dried on the side slats, you can do the final fitting of the crate's bottom. The bottom should be a bit oversized. Don't worry, this was done on purpose. It's always better to have to trim a bit off than to add some on.

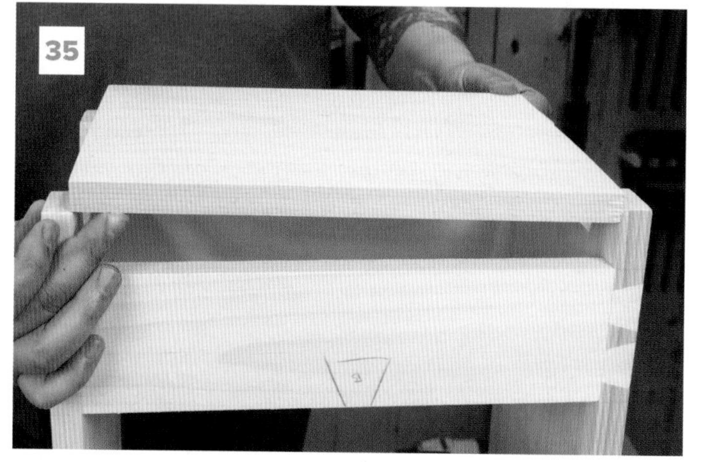

36 Adjust the bottom. Test-fit the bottom then use a bench plane with a sharp blade to trim the piece to fit, as needed.

37 Clean it all up. Once you have the bottom fitting well, take the time to smooth all of the outside surfaces with a smoother. Be sure to finish all the smoothing before installing the bottom because you will be using forged nails to secure the bottom, and nails don't plane very well.

INSTALL THE BOTTOM

38 | **Drill for nails.** The nails I am using here are called clout nails. These nails have an elongated diamond-shaped shaft and a large head, offering incredible holding power. Square-ended nails are less prone to splitting wood as they are driven in because they cut their way in rather than wedging like a wire nail. That being said, a pilot hole is still a smart idea. Pick a drill bit that is just a bit wider than the small end of the nail. This will allow the nail to cut in and secure things without splitting the wood.

39 | **Drive them home.** Tap the nails in with the wide section of the nail running with the grain, again to prevent splitting.

LAY ON THE FINISH

40 Finish it off. With the crate fully assembled, it's time for the finish. When designing these crates, I thought about how I want them to age and patina the way only softwoods can. I want dents and scratches to appear over time. That being said, I do want some surface protection—but nothing too heavy. Here I am using an oil and wax combination that penetrates the surface and leaves a nice appearance. The beauty of these sheer finishes is that they go on easily and can be topped up over the years as needed.

Whether you are storing your covetable vinyl collection, extra extension cords, or some power tools you need to transport, these crates are up for the task. They are easy to carry around and stack nicely to reduce your storage footprint. I bet you can't build just one.

CHAPTER 6

6-BOARD CHEST

This handsome chest features joinery that isn't seen as often as other box-making joints you may know. The pinned lap joints used here are a good alternative to finger joints or dovetails. You'll notice that the construction of this box—and many like it—defies the rules of grain orientation. The end panels have grain that runs vertically while the front and back panels have grain that runs horizontally. This is usually a faux pas in woodworking, but countless examples of this joinery stand the test of time.

The key is to not use glue on these joints and only use nails. As the wood moves throughout the seasons, the nails will allow that movement to happen while still holding everything together. For this chest I decided to use forged clout nails for both purpose and design. These nails have immense holding power and the shape of the head is the look I'm after.

Another nuance to this chest is the use of milk paint. Milk paint has proven to be a durable finish that allows the use of color in your woodworking. Milk paint is quite versatile and can be used to create everything from a wash of color, to an opaque look, to everything in between.

TOOLS

Jack plane
Smoothing plane
Block planes
Rip and crosscut saws
Chisels
Mallet
Marking gauge
Marking knife
Dividers
Chisels
Mallet
Curved spokeshave
Dovetail saw
Coping saw
Sandpaper
Adjustable square
Router plane
Hammer
#8 countersink/pilot bit

CUT LIST

PART	QTY	LENGTH	WIDTH	THICKNESS
Front & Back	2	24"	11"	¾"
Ends	2	14"	11"	¾"
Bottom	1	23-½"	11"	¾"
Lid	1	24"	11"	¾"
Lid batten spacers	2	8-⅜"	1-¾"	¾"
Lid batten stays	2	9-¼"	1-¾"	¼"

MATERIALS

1-½" clout nails
1-½" brad nails
#8 1-½ wood screws
Purple 3M rubbing pads
Milk paint
Shellac
Furniture wax

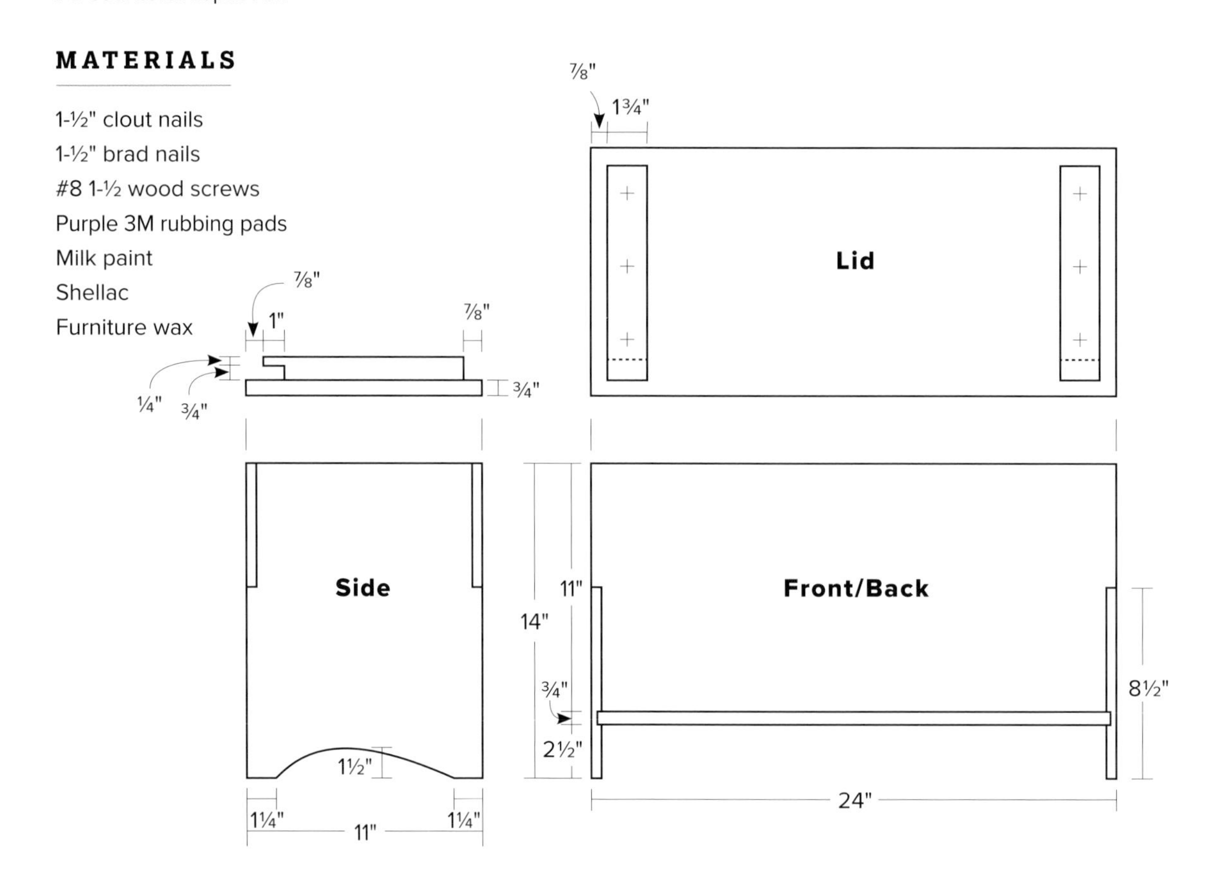

PLAN OUT THE PARTS

1 **Break out the lumber.** Use the dimensions in the cut list, or adjust the sizes to fit your tastes and space. If you change one measurement, just be sure to adjust all the affected dimensions. Take the time to orient the parts so that you pick your inside and outside surfaces, then mark them with a cabinetmaker's triangle to keep them organized.

2 **Lay out the joinery.** Mark out the lap joints on the ends of the front and back pieces, according to the drawing. Find the center of the board's width and make a mark.

3 **Work from a centerline.** Set an adjustable square to the center mark and use it for the rest of the layout. This will ensure that all of your marks are consistent. Also, be sure to reference the top of the box throughout the layout to make sure that things work out. Changing your reference surfaces will lead to confusion and possible errors.

PLAN OUT THE PARTS *(continued)*

4 Lay out the joint. Set a wheel marking gauge to the thickness of your material and strike a depth line on the top halves of the joints.

5 Mark the ends. Be sure to wrap each line around the edge and on to the reverse side.

6 Remember your center-point. Use a knife to go over the center mark so that you have a knife line to reference when cutting the shoulder.

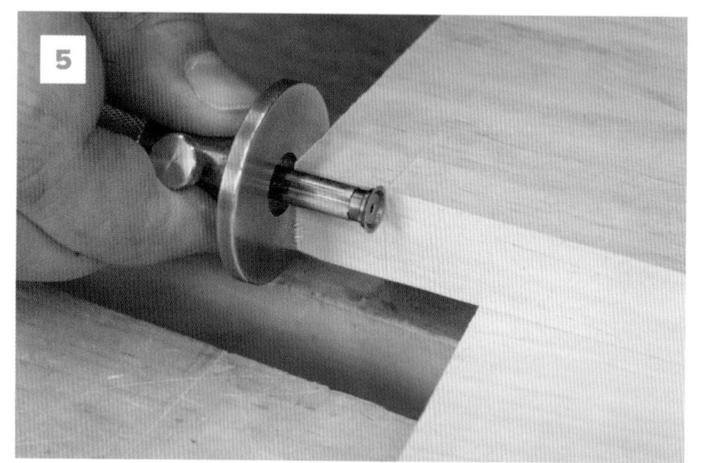

CUT THE CORNER JOINTS

7 | Two for the work of one. I find that clamping the boards together for sawing makes it easier to saw straight.

8 | Keep it straight. Crosscut along the line, placing the kerf line into the waste and stopping at the knife line. Then cut the shoulder of the lap joint along the knife line.

CUT THE CORNER JOINTS *(continued)*

9 | Clean up the saw marks. You can plane this surface true with a block plane. If you happen to have a rabbet block plane, you can use this instead to true up the cut and work into the corner of the adjoining shoulder.

10 | Don't forget the corners. Then work with a paring chisel to get into the tight spots on the inside corners.

11 | Mark the mating joint. Once the lap joints are cut on the front and back, orient the parts, then balance the ends on edge, and lay the appropriate piece (either the front or the back) on them. Ensure that the top edges are lined up then strike a line with a knife to mark the shoulder of the joint. Repeat the layout steps from the first half of the joint to the ends. Then saw out the waste and clean up the joint in the same manner as above.

9

10

11

DADO FOR THE BOTTOM

12 **Mark the dado location.** To accommodate the bottom of the chest, begin by joining the appropriate front or back and end together. Then make a mark on the end board with a knife. This will locate the top surface of the chest's bottom. Do this for each corner of the chest.

13 **Connect the marks.** Then use a straightedge to join the two marks with a knife line.

14 **Establish the dado width.** While leaving the straightedge in place, position an offcut of the bottom material along the straightedge toward the bottom of the chest end and make a mark along its length.

DADO FOR THE BOTTOM *(continued)*

15 | Mark out the waste. These two lines establish the width of the dado. Mark the waste to be removed and strike the depth of the dado (¼").

16 | Work smart, not fast. Don't dive into the dado quite yet. First, locate some nail holes and mark the curve on the bottom of the end pieces. Lay down some blue tape and locate the nail locations so they are evenly spaced.

17 | Drill for the nails. The nails for this application are 1-½" clout nails. These nails have incredible holding power and require a pilot hole so that the wood doesn't crack. In softwood, choose a pilot hole size that allows clearance for the thinnest part of the nail—in this case the pilot hole is ⅛". Drill all the holes required to attach the sides to the ends.

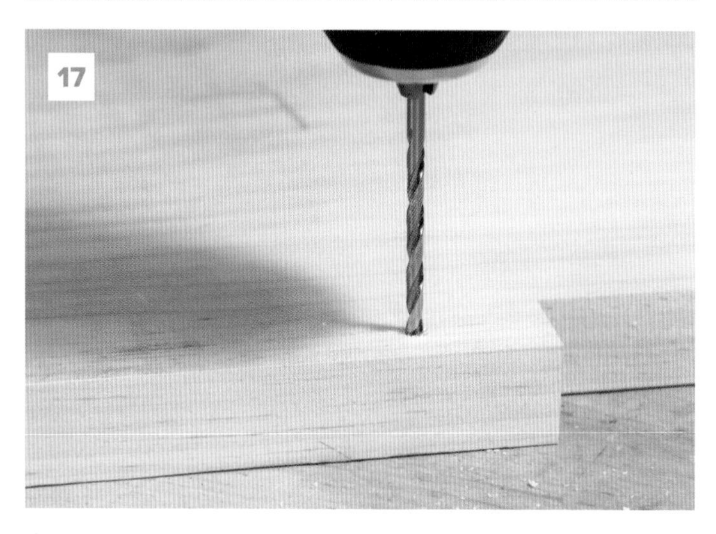

PREPARE THE FEET

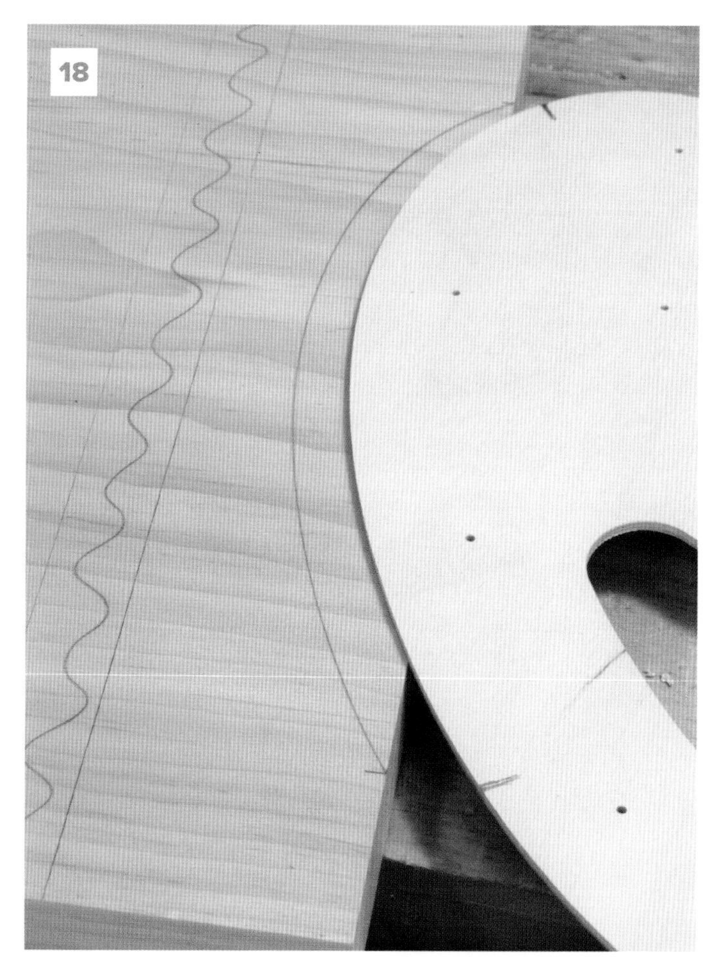

18 | Draw the foot profile. Use a French curve or any curved object that is the correct size to mark the cut-out for the bottom of the end pieces.

19 | Your chest, your design. This cut-out creates four feet for the chest. The shape is largely decorative and subject to personal choice. Historically, these cut-outs would be part of a circle's radius or a gentler curve. I chose to use a French curve to lay out an asymmetric curve to give this chest a bit of a modern twist.

COMPLETE THE DADO CUTS

20 Back to the dadoes. Create a knife wall along the two knife lines that delineate the dado.

21 Tape keeps it safe. Apply blue tape along the dado to protect the wood from getting marked up by the sole of the router. Use a crosscut saw to cut the edges of the dado, stopping just above the final depth.

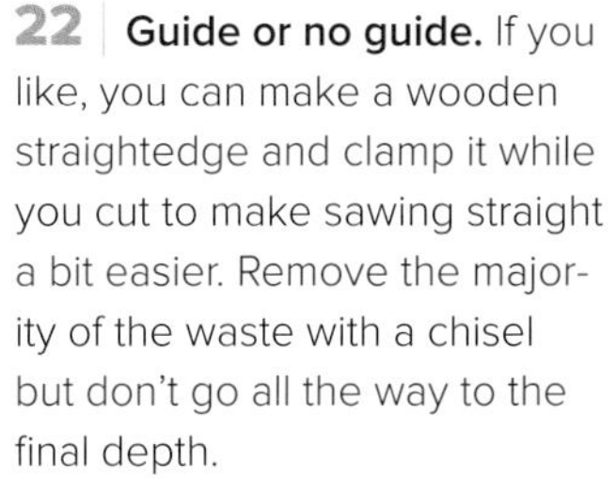

22 **Guide or no guide.** If you like, you can make a wooden straightedge and clamp it while you cut to make sawing straight a bit easier. Remove the majority of the waste with a chisel but don't go all the way to the final depth.

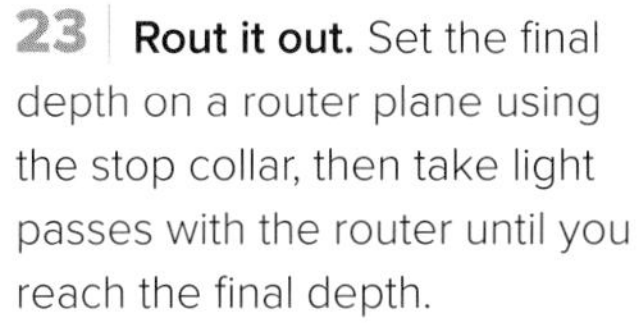

23 **Rout it out.** Set the final depth on a router plane using the stop collar, then take light passes with the router until you reach the final depth.

24 **Keep it clean.** As long as the blade is sharp, a router plane leaves an accurate and clean dado. Use a chisel to clean out any wood fibers that may be left in the corners to ensure that the bottom seats all the way into the dado.

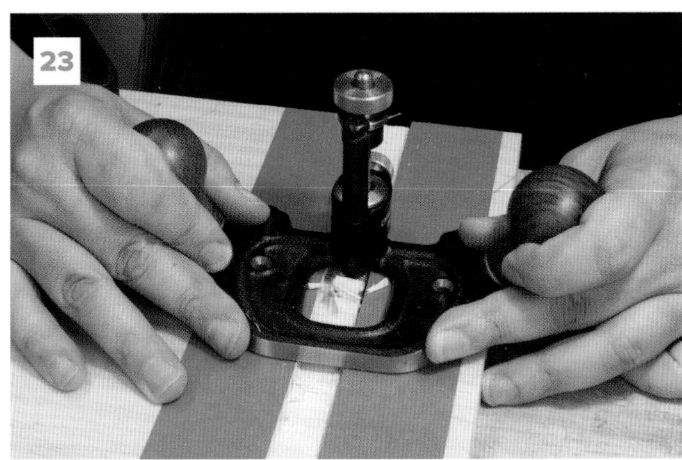

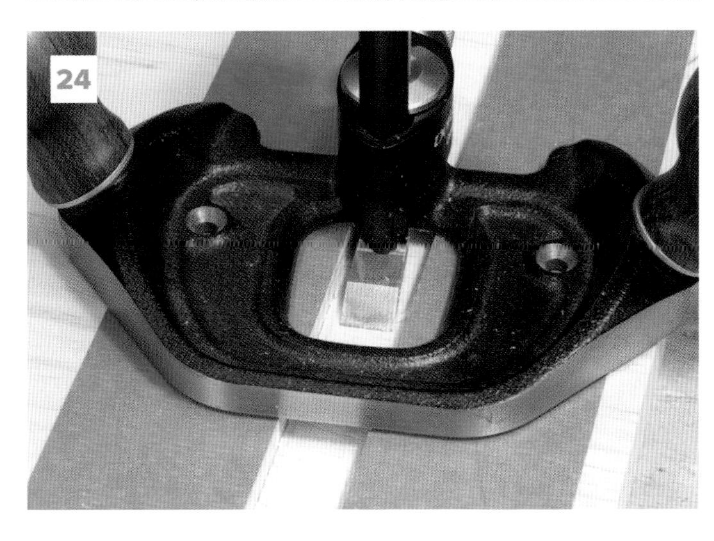

CUT OUT THE CURVED BOTTOM

25 | **Create the feet.** With the dadoes cut, flip the end over and cut out the curved detail on the bottom. A bow saw is a great tool for this task, but if you don't have one you can also get by with a coping saw.

26 | **Smooth out the curve.** Use a curved spokeshave and/or sandpaper until the curve is fair and looks good.

27 | **Sandpaper fairs the cut.** Using a thin piece of wood to back-up the sandpaper will make it easier to smooth out any lumps and bumps.

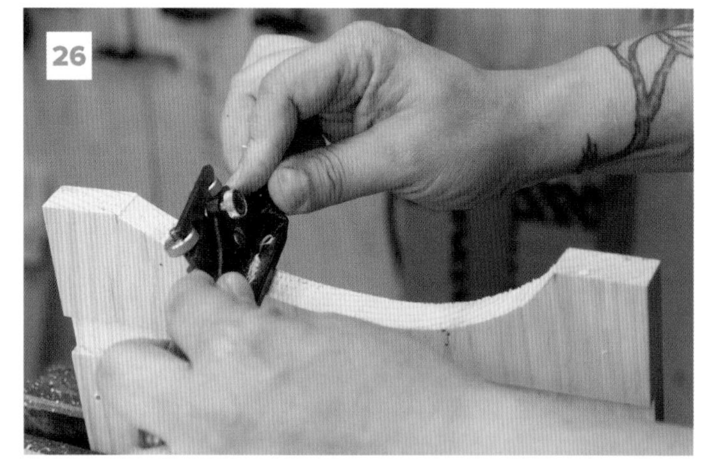

PREPARE FOR FINISHING

28 **Review your work.** With all the joinery cut and the shaping done, it's time to prepare the surfaces for finish. Use a smoothing plane to take off any marks and pencil that may have accumulated on the pieces.

29 **Small touches add a lot.** Create a small, 1⁄16" chamfer on the outside bottom of the front and back pieces and the adjacent corner on the chest's bottom. This small detail will create a small decorative line at the bottom of the chest.

PREPARE FOR FINISHING *(continued)*

30 | Pre-finishing saves time. Before final assembly, apply finish to the inside surfaces. I start with a light coat of shellac. Mix up a half-pound cut of shellac as directed and apply a single coat with a natural-hair brush. Be sure to not overwork the shellac as it dries fairly quickly and you can end up with brush strokes. Lay the shellac down in lines making sure to overlap those lines to get a consistent result.

31 | Wax on, wax off. Once the shellac is dry, apply a thin coat of furniture wax. Allow the wax to set, then buff the wax with a soft cloth.

MIXING SHELLAC

De-waxed shellac is a great product to use as a seal coat. As long as it's wax-free, any finish can be used on top of it. De-waxed shellac can be purchased pre-made or as flakes that you can mix yourself. I prefer to mix my own shellac because then I know how fresh it is. I like using a light-colored shellac, sometimes referred to as blonde shellac, because it won't impart much color to the piece but will still warm the wood up a little.

To mix shellac, all you need are the shellac flakes and some denatured alcohol. Shellac is mixed as a ratio referred to as "pound-cuts"; you mix a certain weight of shellac to a volume of denatured alcohol. For example, one pound (454 grams) of shellac dissolved in one gallon (3.8 liters) of denatured alcohol will yield a one-pound cut of shellac. One- and two-pound cuts are considered light cuts, and three- to four-pound cuts are considered heavy cuts.

All this being said, you certainly don't have to mix up a gallon of shellac. In fact, I highly recommend mixing up small batches to suit your needs so that you are always working with fresh finish. To make one cup of shellac, you will need to dissolve one ounce of shellac flakes with one cup of denatured alcohol. I keep a small food scale in my shop to make the measuring easier, and a Mason jar is great vessel to mix in.

Simply stir the shellac into the alcohol with a wooden stir stick and let it do its thing. Stir the mixture often over the next few hours as it dissolves so that the shellac doesn't end up as a large goopy lump in the bottom of the jar. Once the shellac is fully dissolved, pass it through a paint filter into a clean jar and it's ready to use. Keep a lid on the shellac when it's not in use so that the alcohol doesn't evaporate.

ASSEMBLE THE CHEST

32 **Bring it all together.** With the inside surfaces finished, you can move on to assembly. Just a quick reminder that there is no glue used for the chest. I have found that hand screws are a useful set of extra hands when you assemble the chest. They allow the ends to be held upright while laying the front and back into the correct position.

33 **Clamps are an extra hand.** Use clamps to hold one side in place while you nail the opposite end piece to the sides. The heads of clout nails are meant to be proud so don't try to hammer them flush.

34 **Attach the other side.** Flip the assembly onto the nailed end then attach the other end in the same manner. You may find it easier to do this by standing the assembly on a lower surface such as a sawbench.

ASSEMBLE THE CHEST *(continued)*

35 | Adjust as necessary. Once the sides and ends are all nailed together, slide the bottom in place. If the bottom is a bit too long to fit into the two dadoes, just reduce the length of the bottom with a few plane passes and try again. Keep doing this until the bottom slides into place.

36 | Attach the bottom. Turn the assembly over and nail the bottom to the front and back of the chest using square brad nails and, again, no glue.

37 | Clean the top edge. Flip the chest onto its feet and level any misalignment of the top edges using a handplane.

PREPARE THE LID

38 | **A unique design.** The lid of this box is interesting because it is a lift lid but has a built-in system to rest the lid on the back of the chest. This gets done with the special battens installed on the inside of the lid. These battens also help locate the lid on the chest and prevent it from sliding off. They also help keep the top flat over the years. Mill up the material for the battens and cut them according to the cut list.

39 | **Planed surfaces are best.** Use a smoothing plane to clean up the mating faces on each of the two-piece battens.

40 | **Glue up the battens.** This is the only place we use glue in this project. Glue together the two pieces required to make the battens and clamp them up until the glue sets.

PREPARE THE LID *(continued)*

41 | Locate the battens. Once they are out of the clamps, clean up the batten edges to prepare them for installation. This two-piece construction makes it easy to store the lid on the back of the chest because the thicker of the two pieces creates the standoff required for it to slide into place.

42 | Set them in position. Mark the location for the two battens on the underside of the lid according to the drawing, and lay them in place.

43 & 44 | Lay out the screw placement. Complete the lid by driving three screws through each batten into the top of the lid. For the screw locations, find the center of the battens then mark the hole locations according to the drawing. I marked a centerline, then used dividers to make sure screw placement was the same on both battens.

41

42

43

44

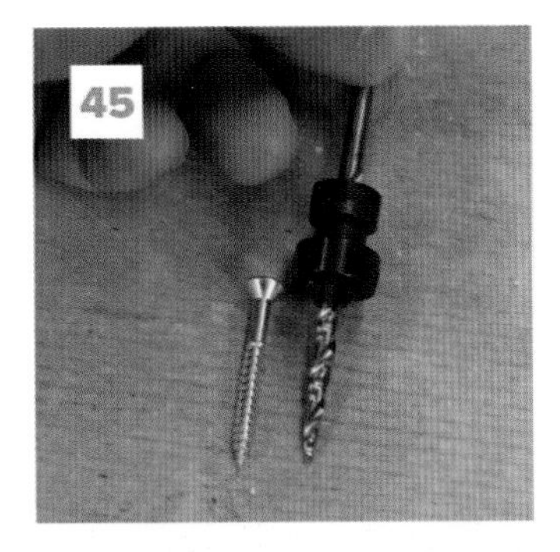

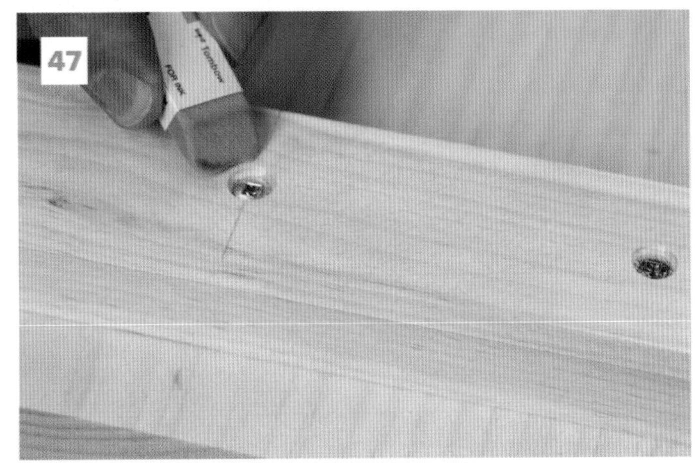

45 & 46 | **Drill for screws.** Use a countersink bit sized for a #8 screw to drill the pilot holes into the battens and lid.

47 | **Install the screws.** Be sure to not use glue at all—you are already breaking the grain direction rules and the wood needs the ability to move. I can assure you that the screws will be enough to hold things in place. To remove any markings, get your hands on an ink eraser and you'll wonder why you haven't used one to erase pencil from wood before.

48 | **Clean up the lid.** Take your time to level off any adjacent surfaces and ease all of the edges with a block plane and/or sandpaper.

PAINT FINISHES IT OFF

49 | **Start with shellac.** Before you move on to milk paint, apply a coat of shellac to all of the outside surfaces.

50 | **Pick a color, any color.** Choosing a color for the milk paint is completely up to you. I chose green for my chest, but I'm also a fan of deep blue and red. Mix the paint according to the manufacturer's instructions and apply it with a brush. Paint only the outside surfaces, leaving the insides natural with shellac only.

51 | **Smooth the surface.** Once the **paint** is dry, it will have an extremely matte look to it and will likely feel a bit rough to the hand. Use a purple 3M rubbing pad to smooth the surfaces, then apply a topcoat to protect the paint.

52 | **Tung oil is a great topcoat** choice because it will add protection to the surface without making it look "candy coated."

Simply coat the surface with a thin layer of tung oil and leave the surface a bit wet. Let the oil sit for about 24 hours then wipe off the remaining oil. Let the chest dry another 24-48 hours and it should be ready for use.

Be careful with the rags you use with tung oil because they can auto combust. The curing process is thermogenic, meaning that it creates heat as it cures—enough heat that balled-up rags can start to smoke and catch fire. A good habit to get into is to find a spot for the rags to hang while they dry—somewhere outside is even better. Once they are dry, they can be thrown away.

CHAPTER 7

HANGING WALL CABINET

"A place for everything and everything in its place" is an old adage that can help us stay organized, and a simple wall cabinet can certainly help with that. The design of this cabinet is modern, with clean lines and simple joinery. The sides are connected to the top and bottom using a series of dowels and the permanent shelf sits in a dado. A couple of new skills will be seen in this project as well: installing hinges and veneering.

Veneering has gotten a bad reputation because it is often associated with cheap disposable furniture. However, done correctly, veneered elements in a piece of furniture can be just as durable as solid-wood components. There are veneered antiques well over 100 years old that are still in great shape! Many woodworkers shy away from working with veneers, but as you're about to see, using them is quite simple and they can add striking elements to your work.

TOOLS

Jack plane
Smoothing plane
Block planes
Rip and crosscut saws
Chisels
Mallet
Marking gauge
Marking knife
Dividers
Chisels
Mallet
Sandpaper
Adjustable square
Router plane
Rabbet plane
Drill bits
Cordless Drill
Flush-cut saw
Veneer press
7⁄16" Forstner bit

MATERIALS

Blue painter's tape
Dowel
Cold-press glue
2 butt hinges, 1-1⁄8"

CUT LIST

PART	QTY	MATERIAL	LENGTH	WIDTH	THICKNESS
Side	2	Walnut	19"	5-3⁄4"	5⁄8"
Top and bottom	2	Walnut	11"	5-3⁄4"	5⁄8"
Fixed shelf	1	Walnut	11-1⁄2"	5-1⁄2"	1⁄2"
Adjustable shelf	1	Walnut	11"	5-1⁄2"	1⁄2"
Door substrate	1	Baltic birch ply	18-15⁄16"	12-1⁄8"	5⁄8"
Banding	4	Walnut	20"	3⁄4"	1⁄8"
Veneer	2	Maker's choice	19-3⁄16"	12-3⁄8"	
Back	1	Baltic birch ply	18-3⁄8"	11-9⁄16"	6mm

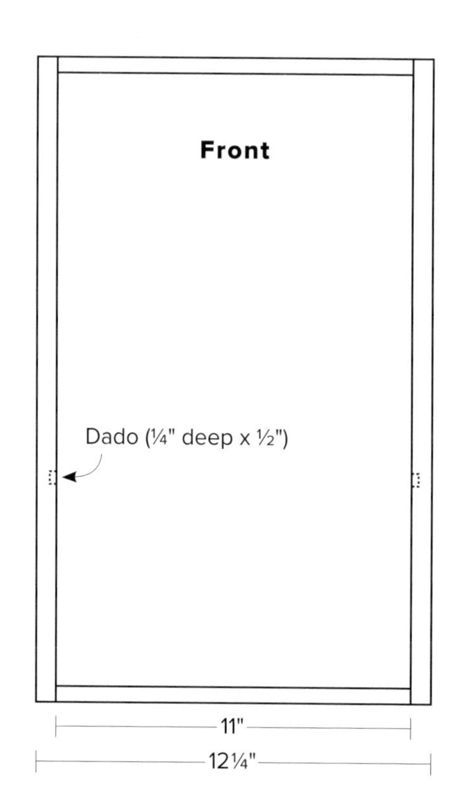

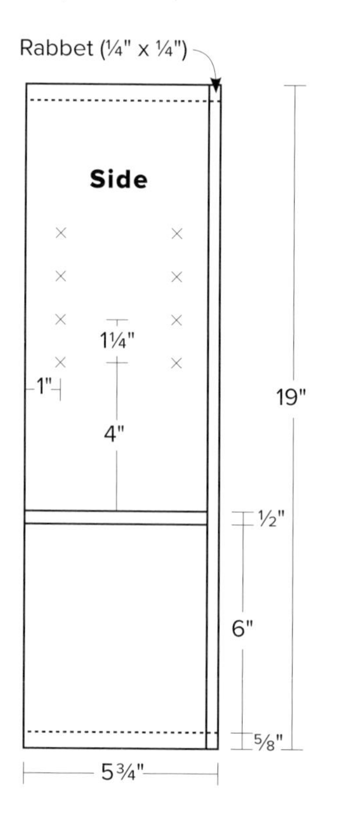

PLAN OUT THE PARTS

1 Choose your materials. Begin by breaking out the lumber according to the cut list and prepare the material to final sizes. Mark the part arrangement using cabinetmaker's triangles. Leave the shelf pieces a bit long so that you can fit them later.

2 Set up your rabbet plane. The back of the cabinet is set in rabbets cut on the rear edges of all four pieces of the carcase. The back panel is 6mm thick Baltic birch plywood, so the rabbet will have to be 6mm (¼") deep. You can make the width of the rabbet ¼", as well, so set your rabbet plane's depth stop and fence both at ¼".

If you are thinking ahead, you may reckon that the through-rabbets on all the pieces will create a gap on the top and bottom of the cabinet corners. Don't worry about this. No one will ever see them when the cabinet is on the wall.

Make sure that your rabbet plane is set up well. The corner of the blade should be set so that it is protruding just a pigeon hair (no more than 1/64"), from the side of the plane. This will ensure that you don't end up with a stepped rabbet. Also, make sure that the blade is set so that the edge is parallel to the front of the mouth. This will keep the rabbet flat on the bottom.

CUT THE CARCASE JOINERY

3 | A built-in steering wheel. Place the fingers of your steering hand on the fence and use a loose grip with your pushing hand. This helps keep the plane cutting true and will help prevent you from tilting it in use. Start at the front of the cut and remove a couple of inches of material. Then bring the plane a few inches back and push forward for another cut. Inch your way back until you are making a full-length cut. Once you have a full-length cut, continue making them until you reach the depth stop on the plane. This technique helps keep the plane cutting straight.

You'll notice that I have removed the front knob of this plane. I've done this because I feel the plane is more "tippy" if you grab onto this knob, and the easiest way to prevent grabbing it is to remove it altogether.

4 | Mark out the dadoes. The fixed shelf in this cabinet is housed in dadoes cut into the sides. Whenever I lay out cabinet joinery, I like to clamp the sides together and mark them as one. This helps to reduce measuring and transfer errors.

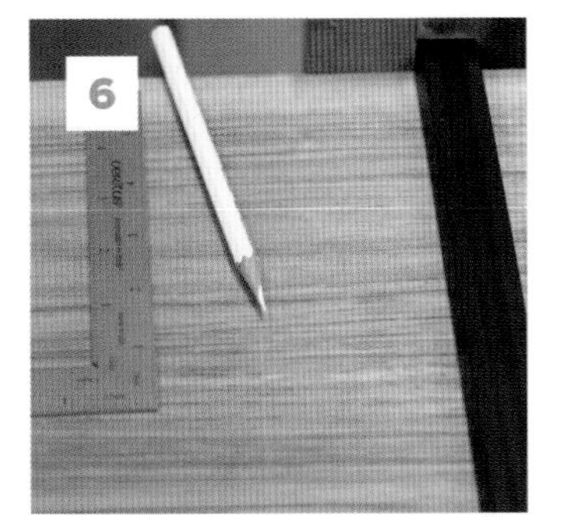

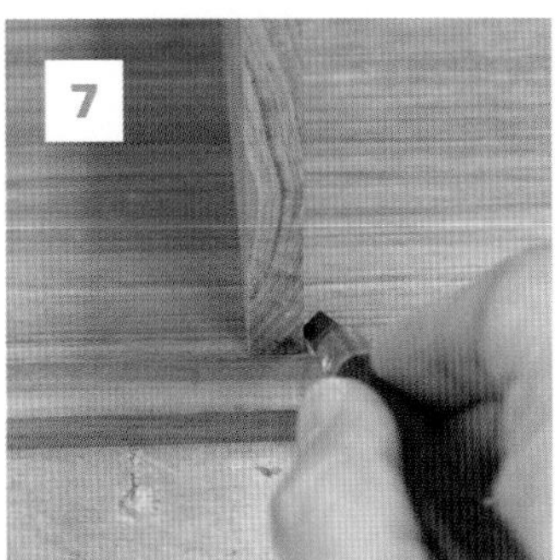

5 Determine the shelf location. Measure up from the bottom of the side according to the drawing and mark the location with a pencil.

6 Extend your mark. Carry the pencil line across the two sides of the cabinet using a square.

7 Mark off the shelf itself. Lay the shelf material onto the pencil line and mark the shelf's thickness using a marking knife. Then carry those knife lines across the sides. Start with light passes with the knife so that you don't accidentally stray from the straight edge.

8 The dadoes are stopped. Locate the stop location at the front of the sides according to the drawing. This will hide the dado at the front of the cabinet, giving it a clean look. The depth of the dado will match the depth of the rabbet you cut earlier, so no need to mark that.

CUT THE CARCASE JOINERY

9 | **Chisel it out.** Cutting this dado is a bit different than cutting a through dado, mainly because you aren't able to use a saw to cut the walls. Instead, use a chisel to cut straight down into the knife lines that you made. Then, hold the chisel at a low angle to remove a piece of material.

10 | **Work slow and steady.** You're essentially creating a progressively deeper knife wall until you hit the bottom of the dado. Don't drive the chisel too deep when you are making the wall cuts. This will drive the chisel past the knife line, creating a dado wider than you want.

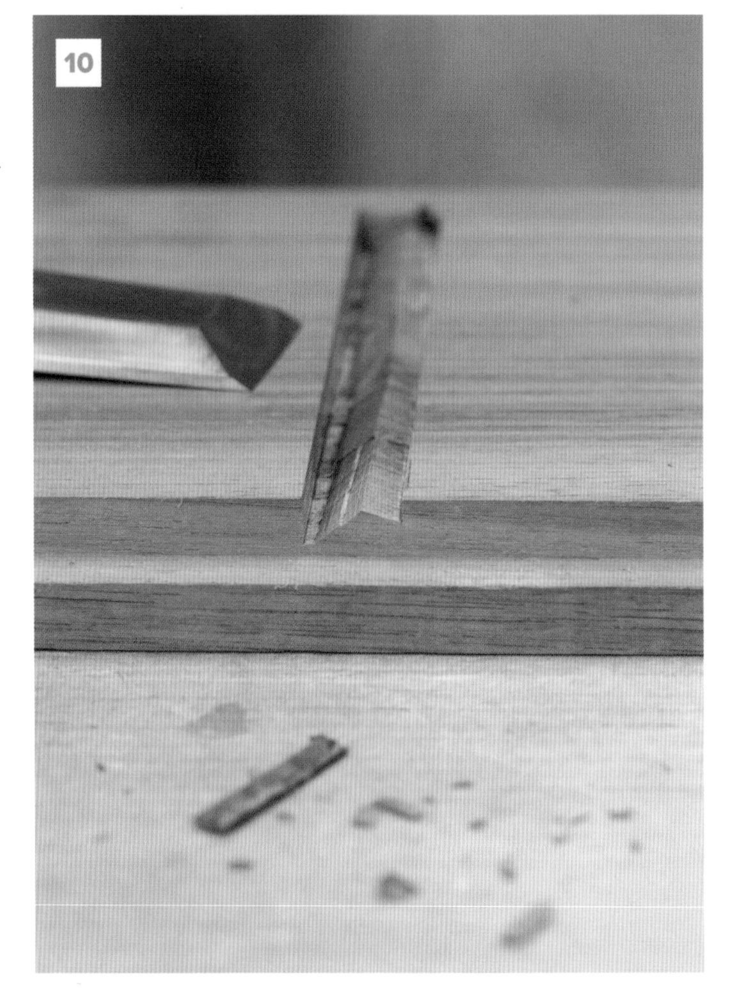

11 | Chisel out the waste. Once you are at depth (or close to it), pick a chisel that is slightly narrower than your dado and hog out the majority of the waste.

12 | Keep the ends crisp. Finish off the chisel work by removing any waste vertically at the dado stop.

13 | Smooth the dado bottom. Set a router plane to the final depth and pare out the bottom of the dado.

ADD AN ADJUSTABLE SHELF

14 | **An optional shelf.** To add an adjustable shelf, lay out holes for shelf pins. Lay blue tape down to protect the surface and locate the holes according to the drawing. The shelf will rest on shelf pins, and sometimes those pins come with sleeves to protect the surrounding wood. If you are using sleeves, drill deep enough to ensure that they can be set just below the surface.

15 | **Set up your drill.** Pick a drill bit to match the pin or sleeve. I'm using a commonly available jig for drilling holes perpendicular to the surface, and a stop collar to control the depth.

16 | **Not too deep.** Be careful when setting the depth—you don't want to drill through the cabinet side. Once you are ready to go, drill your holes.

14

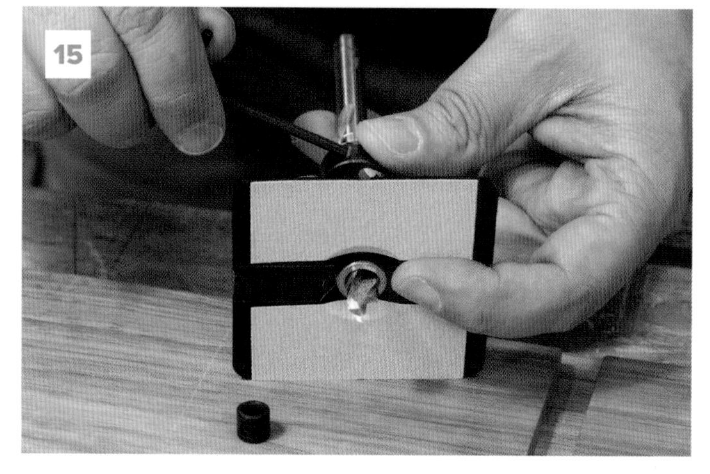
15

16

ASSEMBLE THE CASE

17 | Create a quick doweling jig. The case will be assembled using dowels. Holes for those dowels will be made with a simple jig that you will make for this one project, then discard. You might be wondering why you can't keep this jig if you want to make this cabinet more than once. I recommend discarding the jig each time because the drill bit can wear the jig out, throwing off your layout. The interesting thing about this jig is that, when used correctly, it ensures that the two pieces mate correctly, even if the holes are a bit off.

Start by cutting hardwood to create the jig. The jig should be the same thickness as your cabinet sides and extra-long to have enough material for the fence. Lay the stock down along the width of the side and mark it with a pencil.

18 | Cut and square the ends. Cut at the pencil line and true the cut up with a plane.

ASSEMBLE THE CASE *(continued)*

19 | **Drill through the jig.** Mark the hole locations with 1 ¼" spacing between each, then drill the holes into the jig.

20 | **Remove the sharp edges.** Chamfer the holes on both sides of the jig using a countersink,

21 | **You'll need to attach it.** Drill clearance holes for the #4 screws that will hold the jig in place during use. To help locate the jig on the workpieces, glue the fence on to the jig using thick CA glue.

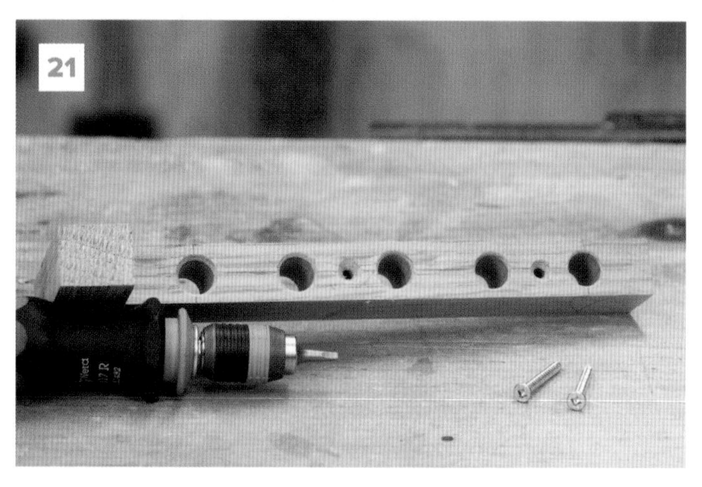

22

23

22 | **Keep everything organized.** The key to using this jig effectively is marking a cabinetmaker's triangle on the jig in the correct orientation. Then it is as simple as matching up the triangle orientation on the jig with the marks on the cabinet parts. Work on the sides first. Line up the jig so that it is flush with the end of the side and the fence is against the front of the cabinet. Once it's lined up, screw the jig in place. Don't worry about the holes left by the screws because they will be hidden once the case is assembled.

23 | **Set the depth.** Use a stop collar set the correct depth. The bit should go no closer than ⅛" from poking out the other side.

ASSEMBLE THE CASE *(continued)*

24 | **It's time to drill.** Using the holes in the jig as your guide, drill all the holes into the sides of the carcase.

25 | **Clean up the holes.** Chamfer the edges of the holes using a countersink. With the sides done, repeat the process with the top and bottom pieces. You can drill the holes deeper in the top and bottom, so have the drill bit set to drill down 1".

26 | **Stay organized.** Again, make sure the triangle on the jig matches the triangles on the cabinet components. This marks the end of the carcass joinery.

24

25

26

PREPARE PARTS FOR FINISH

27 **Work smart.** Before anything is assembled, prepare all of the parts for finish with a smoother.

28 **Get ready for shelves.** If your shelf pins require it, insert the sleeves that hold them in place.

29 **Set the dowels in place.** Add a drop of glue into each of the holes, then set the dowels into the top and bottom of the carcase sides. Trim the dowels to length, if needed.

PREPARE PARTS FOR FINISH *(continued)*

30 | **Work out the kinks.** Get some clamps and do a dry assembly to make sure everything works well.

31 | **Prepare the shelf.** Place the shelf in place and mark the final length. Then make the cut and adjust it until you have a snug fit that won't bow the carcase sides.

32

33

34

32 Set it in place. Once the shelf fits, flip the assembly over and place it down onto a couple of pieces of softwood to raise it off the benchtop. Mark the location of the stop onto the front of the shelf with a knife.

33 Determine the shelf setback. Set a marking gauge to the depth of the stop.

34 Mark the shelf to width. Then mark the depth along one edge of the shelf.

PREPARE PARTS FOR FINISH *(continued)*

35 | **Notch the shelf end.** To slide the shelf in place, you need to notch the leading edge. Start by creating a knife wall on the front of the shelf.

36 | **Saw to the line.** Saw to the knife wall using a crosscut saw.

37 | **Clean it up.** True things up with a chisel if necessary. You can also fit the adjustable shelf by making sure it slides easily into the cabinet and that it doesn't protrude past the edge of the cabinet's front.

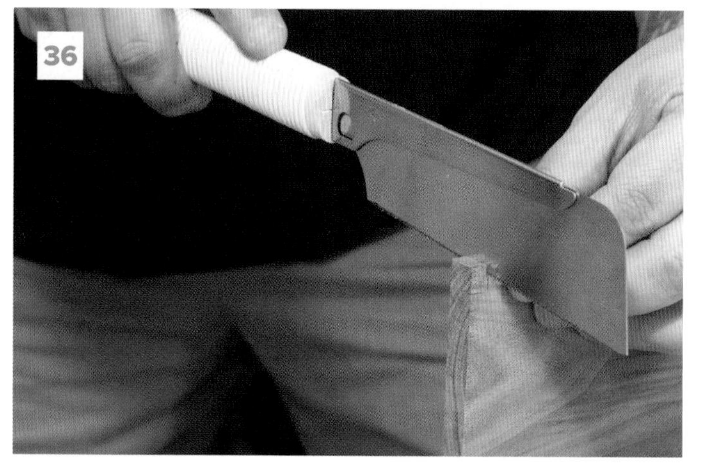

38 | It's time for glue to flow. Because you already did a dry test-assembly, all your clamps should be sorted and ready to go. Glue the dowels into the top and bottom pieces, then apply glue to the holes in the sides.

39 | Get ready for the shelf. It only requires a little glue in the front of the dado to hold the shelf in place.

40 | Double-check your work. Clamp the assembly together and check the corners with a square. With the carcass glued up, it's time to move on to making the door.

MAKE THE DOOR

41 | **Use a plywood core.** Consult the cut list and cut the door out of the Baltic birch plywood. You need to be sure that the grain is running in the correct direction on the plywood. This is essential in order to prevent the door from warping. The plies of plywood run 90° to each other alternately, so you have to keep that pattern going. The plywood grain will run across the width of the door and the veneer grain will run vertically. Saw close to your layout lines then true up your cuts with a jack plane. The door will have banding attached to the outside perimeter of the plywood. This will conceal the plies and will make the door edges more durable. Mill up some material according to the cut list and plane it to final dimension.

42 | **Use a quick thicknessing jig.** I made a simple jig to help get consistent thicknesses as I worked. At this point, you can keep the bandings a little oversized so you can trim them later.

41

42

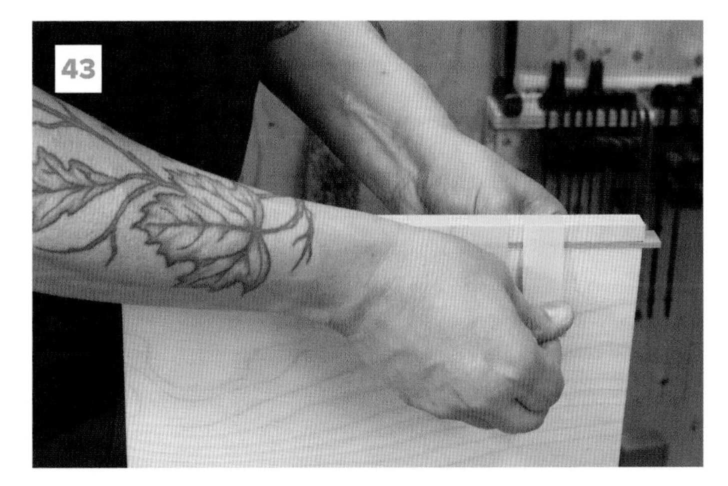

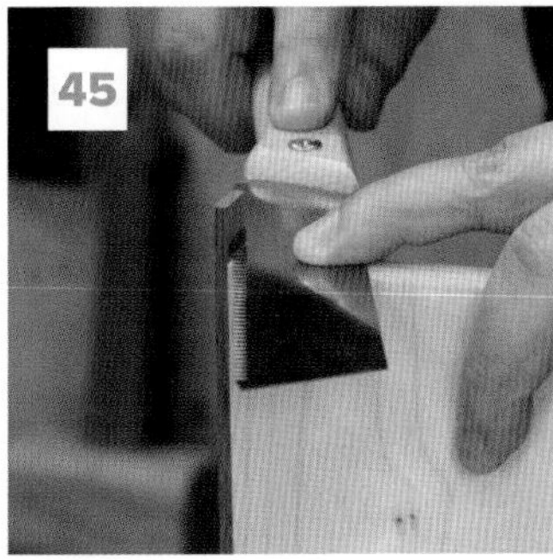

43 | Cauls are extra hands. Make a set of clamping cauls out of Baltic birch plywood to help spread the pressure. Clamping pressure radiates out at an angle around 45° so increasing the distance between the clamp and the glue line will help. In this case, I recommend using tape as a clamp. The tape I'm using here is a 3M product called 233+ and sometimes gets sold as binding tape. Many luthiers use this product because it has great tack but doesn't leave residue behind. There is also quite a bit of stretch to this tape, so you can pull it and attach it in place which will apply clamping pressure.

44 | Band the edges. Start by banding the top and bottom of the door, then let the glue set up for a couple of hours. After the glue has set, remove the tape and use a finely set plane to level the banding with the plywood.

45 | Trim as needed. Use a flush-cutting saw to trim the excess length flush with the plywood.

46 | Finish off the door. Now do the vertical edges of the door using the same techniques. Once this is done, the door substrate is ready for veneer.

MAKE THE DOOR *(continued)*

47 Choose your veneer. The fun part about using veneer is that you can find some unique and interesting pieces that you normally wouldn't find in solid wood. The veneer I'm using is bird's-eye maple with an interesting brown staining in it. If this is your first time veneering, then I highly recommend using a veneer that is wide enough to cover the whole door. Stitching multiple veneers together is an extra level of complexity that you don't need your first-time around.

48 Cut it to size. Place the door onto the veneer and cut out what you need using the door as a pattern. There are many ways to cut veneers, but I find the easiest way to do it is with an Olfa-style knife. Make multiple light cuts with the knife so that you stay on track. I normally take about a dozen strokes to get through the thickness of a veneer. Don't rush this step—take your time and you will get a nice clean edge. Be sure to cut two pieces of veneer, one for the front and one for the back of the door.

47

48

49 | Create veneering cauls. You will need to make two cauls to aid with the pressing. The top caul is a piece of ⅛" tempered Masonite and the bottom is a piece of plywood. The Masonite caul should be covered on one side with packing tape to prevent the glue from sticking.

The bottom caul doesn't need tape because you will only be applying glue and veneer on one side for now.

50 & 51 | Plane and file. Round the outside edges of the cauls so that they aren't so sharp that they can dig into your veneer bag.

MAKE THE DOOR *(continued)*

52 | Stack it up. Essentially you will be making a sandwich that is arranged from bottom to top: plywood caul, door, veneer, and Masonite caul.

First things first, tidy up your workbench of any extra tools, shavings, and other detritus. You have to work efficiently when veneering so don't work in a messy space where things can get knocked off your bench or tripped over. Place a veneer onto one surface of the plywood, lining it up so it is positioned squarely on the substrate. Use blue tape to tape one edge of the veneer down. This tape will also act as a hinge, allowing you to move the veneer like turning a page in a book.

Turn the veneer so that you can see the plywood substrate and apply glue. Go lightly on the glue because you can easily use too much.

53 | Keep the glue coming. Spread out the glue into a uniform thin layer using a brayer. A brayer is a roller normally used for spreading ink for printing, but it does an excellent job with glue as well. Add more glue to any dry areas and continue to roll it out with the brayer.

52

53

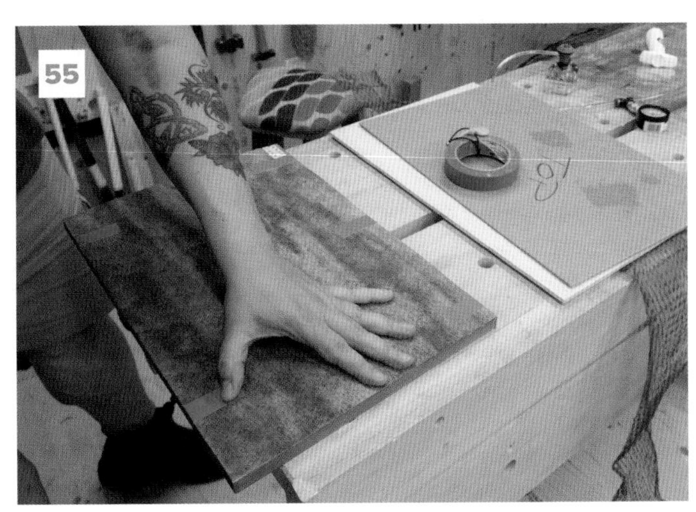

54 **Build up the layers.** Once you have a uniform thin layer, lay the veneer onto the plywood.

55 **Tape it up.** Add a few pieces of blue tape to hold everything in place before it goes into the bag.

VENEER PRESS

We will be using a vacuum bag system called a Thin-Air Press, made by a company in Toronto, Canada, called Roarockit. The kit is simple and inexpensive, and does a great job at veneering many furniture and small box-sized projects. The kit consists of a sealable bag, a hand pump, and some mesh netting. I've used this press for many years and have come to depend on it as a reliable veneer press. My kit has some added features like a remote pumping station and an air pressure gauge, but the basic kit will do just fine. The company also has many resources on how to use its products.

MAKE THE DOOR *(continued)*

56 | **Protect your work.** Place the plywood with veneer onto the bottom caul then add the top caul and secure with more tape to hold the sandwich all together.

57 | **Apply the netting.** Then, wrap the breather net around the whole thing to ensure that all the air will be evacuated from the bag.

58 | **Bag it up.** Place the whole thing into the vacuum bag and seal the bag well with the included butyl rubber tape. Now you simply have to pump out the air with the included pump until you hear the pump make a clicking noise. This should only take a minute or so. Occasionally try to pump out more air for the first 15 minutes or so to make sure you have a good seal. Double-check the butyl rubber, especially at the edges, to make sure all is good.

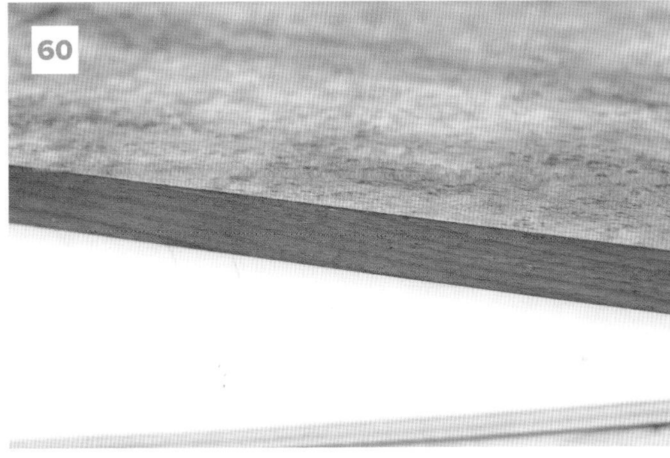

59 | Let the glue set up. Keep the door in the press for at least two hours, then repeat the same process on the other side. If you time things right, you can press the first side, press the second side, then leave it in the bag overnight. Once you remove the door from the bag for the final time, leave it rest for 24 hours so that the glue can finish curing. Once the glue is cured, use a flat file to remove any extra veneer from the edges and to gently round over the edges. The water in the glue can cause the veneers to grow slightly. This is normal and nothing to worry about.

60 | The end result. What you're left with is a nice cabinet door that will make your project look beautiful.

INSTALL THE BACK

61 | Clean up the end grain. Now turn your attention back to the cabinet carcass. Go over the surfaces and make sure that everything is level, including the ends. Place the cabinet onto its front and use the rabbets to size the 6mm Baltic birch plywood for the back.

62 | Install the back. Once the back fits nicely, sand the face of the plywood to #220-grit. Then, put some glue into the rabbet and lay the back in.

63 | Tack the back in place. Use small finish nails to keep everything secure while the glue dries.

ADD THE HANGER

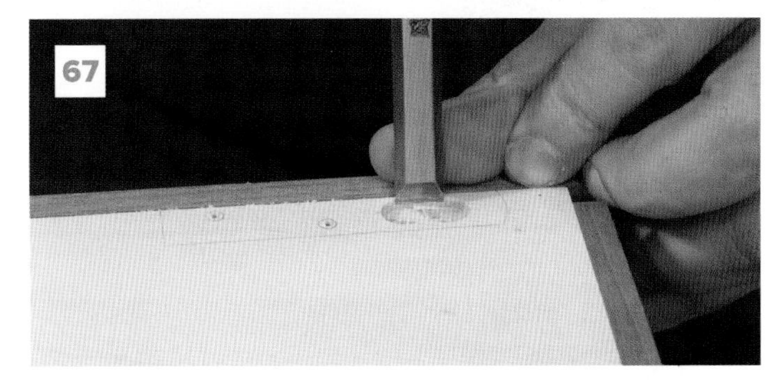

64 **Mark for hanger hardware.** The cabinet will be installed on the wall using a piece of hardware called a keyhole hanger. As the name suggests, the hanger has a keyhole-shaped hole cut into it which will allow a screw head to register in it and lock into place.

65 **Install the hangers.** Locate the top of the hardware 1" from the top of the cabinet and trace the key and screw holes with a pencil. Then bisect the keyhole with a vertical line and mark the center of the screw holes.

66 **Make room for a screw.** Use a 7⁄16" Forstner bit to drill a clearance area for the head of a screw to fit and no deeper.

67 **It takes two.** Then drill a second hole slightly overlapping the first hole and use a chisel to remove the waste, creating an elongated hole. Once you've done this for both hangers, it's time to mount the hangers using screws.

68 **Customize your screws.** Before installing the screws, be sure to shorten them with a mill file to no more than 5mm long to make sure that they don't poke through the back into the cabinet.

INSTALL THE HINGES

69 | Locate the hinges. The last big job for this project is hinging the door. Position the hinges one-hinge length away from the top and bottom of the cabinet, and make a tick with your marking knife. Leave the knife in the tick and push the hinge up against the knife then make a tick mark on the other end of the hinge.

70 | Transfer your marks. Carry the knife marks across the side's edge (with a pencil, for now).

71 | Grab your marking gauge. Set a marking gauge from the edge of the hinge to the middle of the barrel, then mark the hinge width between the two pencil marks.

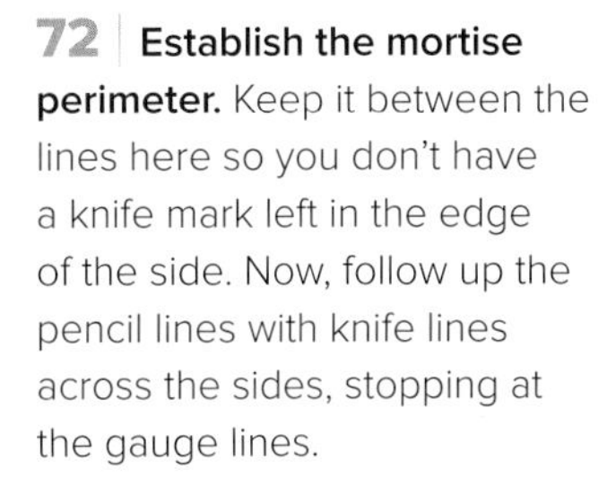

72 | Establish the mortise perimeter. Keep it between the lines here so you don't have a knife mark left in the edge of the side. Now, follow up the pencil lines with knife lines across the sides, stopping at the gauge lines.

73 | Mark the hinge depth. To get your depth, use a wheel marking gauge to mark half the barrel thickness and mark it on the side.

74 | Make a series of cuts. Begin removing the waste by creating a series of chop marks in the waste with a chisel, being mindful not to go too deep, beyond the depth line.

75 | Don't blow out the mortise edge. It's a good idea to clamp a block onto the inside of the side to help support the remaining bit of wood on the edge. This is only about 1⁄16" thick and has a nasty habit of breaking off while you're chiseling.

INSTALL THE HINGES *(continued)*

76 | **Chisel out the bulk of the waste.** Be sure your chisel is sharp. Dull chisels require more force to cut and too much force here will blow out wood you don't want to touch.

77 & 78 | **Grab your router plane.** Set a router plane to your final depth and remove the remaining waste, leaving a flat and even hinge mortise.

76

77

78

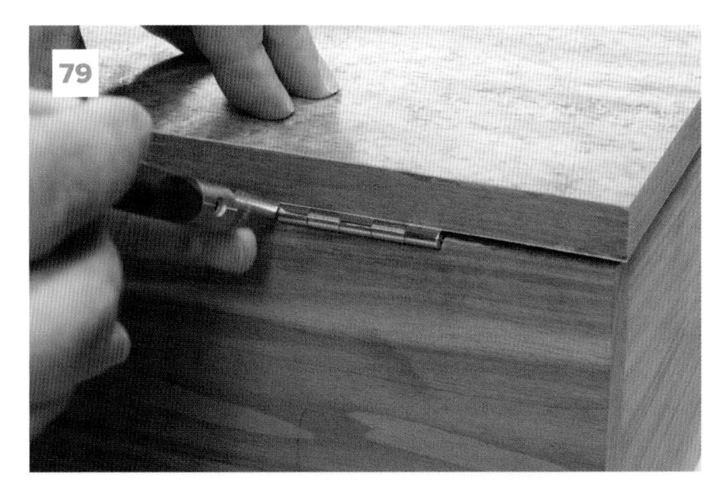

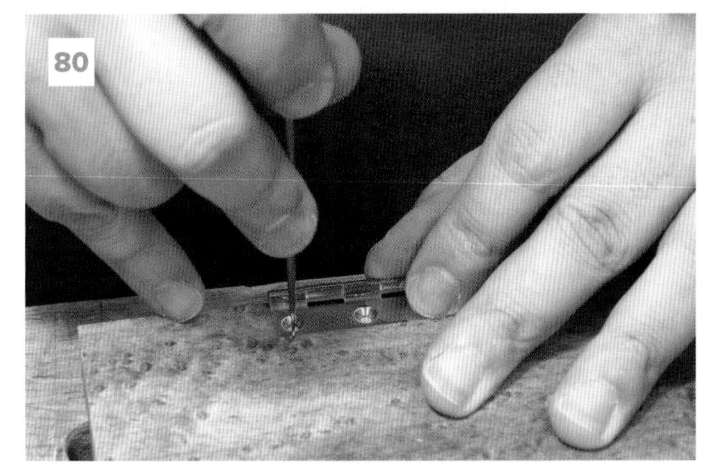

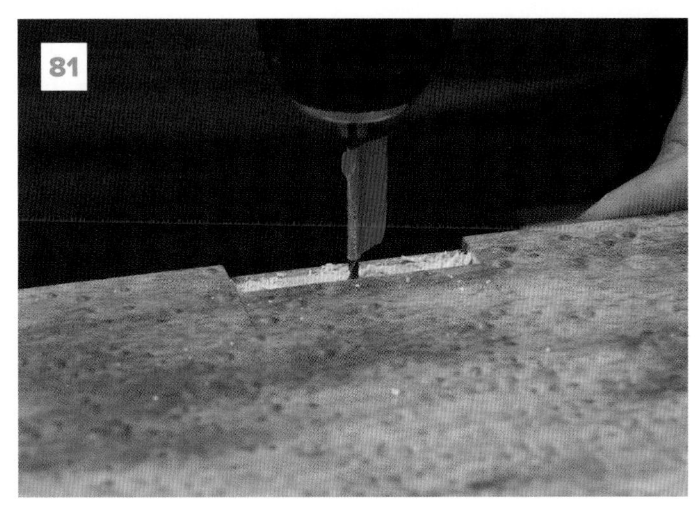

79 | **Locate the hinge.** That's half of the hinge let in. Now place the door onto the case and line up the left edge of the door with the left edge of the case. The door should overlap the case slightly on the right, top, and bottom edges, which is good. This feature will allow you to open the cabinet by sliding your fingers across to catch the door and open it. This makes it so there is no knob or pull required. Put your marking knife against the hinge barrel and mark the edge of the hinge location on the door. Mark the door just as you did with the side and remove the waste.

80 | **Mark for screws.** Lay the hinges in place on the cabinet and mark the hole locations for the screw pilot holes, then do the same on the door using an awl.

81 | **Drill the pilot holes.** Use a bit appropriately sized for the screws that came with the hinges. Be mindful of the thickness of the door—you don't want to drill through the door. Just as you did with the hanger screws, you may end up having to shorten your screws slightly with a mill file to make sure they don't poke through.

INSTALL THE HINGES *(continued)*

82 & 83 | **Install the screws.** Once you make sure everything works as it should, then remove the screws to finish the cabinet.

84 & 85 | **Finish it off.** The final step, as with most projects, is to add a protective finish. In this case I have opted for a wax only finish on the inside and an oil and wax combination for the outside. I did this because oil products can sometimes cause an odor when used on the inside of projects. If you are using an oil product, be sure that you allow any rags to dry prior to throwing them out.

A cabinet of this size is perfect for storing kitchen items like tea or spices, but you can use it for just about anything. For me, this cabinet will likely end up in my shop close to my workbench to store my often-reached-for tools.

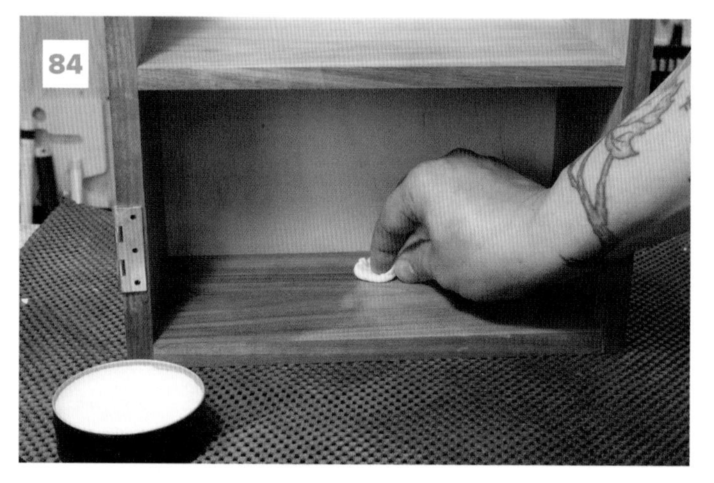

INDEX

Album Crate, *83–101*
- about: overview of, 83; tools/materials and cut list, 84
- assembling crate, 98–99
- assembling joints, 92–93
- creating handle, 96–97
- finishing, 101
- installing bottom, 100
- laying out/cutting tails, 87–88, 89–91
- marking out mating joinery, 89–91
- prepping stock, 85–86
- shaping sides, 94–95

block plane. *See* plane (block)

chest. *See* 6-Board Chest
chisels, projects using. *See* Album Crate; Dovetailed Box; Hanging Wall Cabinet; Perch Stool; 6-Board Chest; Violin Knife

dado cuts and joinery. *See* Hanging Wall Cabinet; 6-Board Chest
dividers, projects using. *See* Dovetailed Box; 6-Board Chest
Dovetailed Box, *36–55*
- about: overview and wood selection, 63; tools/materials and cut list, 64
- gluing it up, 49–50
- laying out parts, 38
- marking/cutting pins, 44-46
- marking/cutting tails, 39–43
- preparing top and bottom, 51-54
- test and fine-tune fit, 48–49

dovetails
- about: anatomy of, illustrated, 37
- projects to practice making. *See* Album Crate; Dovetailed Box; Perch Stool; 6-Board Chest

dowel joints, 68, 78, 137, 141
dowelling jig, 133
drill, cordless
- about: features, reasons for using, 9
- projects using. *See also* Album Crate; Hanging Wall Cabinet; Perch Stool; 6-Board Chest
- using stop collar with, 132, 135

drilling jig, 68, 78. *See also* dowelling jig

files. *See* rasps and files

hand tools
- about: this book, projects and, 8–9
- importance of project for learning to use, 6–7

Hanging Wall Cabinet, *125–57*
- about: overview of, 125; tools/materials and cut list, 126; veneering and, 125
- adding adjustable shelf, 132
- adding hanger, 151
- assembling case, 133–36
- cutting carcase joinery (dadoes), 128–31
- installing back, 150
- installing hinges, 152–57
- making door, 142–49
- planning out parts, 127
- preparing parts for finish, 137–41
- veneer selection, cutting, install, 144–49

hinges, installing, 152–57

jack plane. *See* plane (jack)

knife, marking. *See* marking gauge/knife
knife, violin. *See* Violin Knife

lap joints. *See* 6-Board Chest

mallet, projects using. *See* Album Crate; Dovetailed Box; Hanging Wall Cabinet; Perch Stool; 6-Board Chest; Violin Knife
marking gauge/knife, projects using. *See* Album Crate; Dovetailed Box; Hanging Wall Cabinet; Perch Stool; 6-Board Chest; Violin Knife; Wooden Plane
mortise and tenons, creating. *See* Perch Stool
mortises, for knife blade, 15–17

Perch Stool, *57–81*
- about: inspiration and design, 37; tools/materials and cut list, 38; wood selection, 37
- assembling, 77–81
- create matching feet, 71–73
- creating dowel joint, 67–68
- cutting arch in footrest, 74
- cutting dovetail, 69–70
- mortise for legs, 60
- planning out parts, 59
- shaping seat, 75–76

tenons: cutting, 63–64; marking out and cutting, 62; rounding over, 65
plane (block), projects using. *See* Album Crate; Dovetailed Box; Hanging Wall Cabinet; Perch Stool; 6-Board Chest; Wooden Plane
plane (jack), projects using. *See* Album Crate; Dovetailed Box; Hanging Wall Cabinet; Perch Stool; 6-Board Chest; Wooden Plane
plane (router), projects using. *See* Hanging Wall Cabinet; 6-Board Chest; Violin Knife
plane (smoothing), projects using. *See* Album Crate; Dovetailed Box; Hanging Wall Cabinet; Perch Stool; 6-Board Chest; Violin Knife
plane, building wooden. *See* Wooden Plane
projects
about: dual purpose of, 8; importance of for learning to use tools, 6–7; overview of, 8–9
Album Crate, *83–101*
Dovetailed Box, *37–55*
Hanging Wall Cabinet, *125–57*
Perch Stool, *57–81*
6-Board Chest, *103–23*
Violin Knife, *11–21*
Wooden Plane, *23–35*

rabbet plane, projects using. *See* Album Crate; Dovetailed Box; Hanging Wall Cabinet
rasps and files, projects using. *See* Perch Stool; Violin Knife; Wooden Plane
router plane. *See* plane (router)
saw (bow), project using. *See* Perch Stool
saw (coping), projects using. *See* Album Crate; Dovetailed Box; Perch Stool; 6-Board Chest; Violin Knife
saw (cross cut), projects using. *See* Album Crate; Dovetailed Box; Hanging Wall Cabinet; Perch Stool; 6-Board Chest; Wooden Plane
saw (dovetail), projects using. *See* Dovetailed Box; Perch Stool
saw (rip), projects using. *See* Album Crate; Dovetailed Box; Hanging Wall Cabinet; Perch Stool; 6-Board Chest; Violin Knife; Wooden Plane
shellac, mixing/applying, 116, 122
6-Board Chest, *103–23*
about: milk paint use, 103; mixing shellac for, 116; overview of, 103; tools/materials and cut list, 104
assembling, 117–19
cutting corner joints, 107–8
cutting out curved bottom, 114
dado cuts, 112–13
dado for the bottom, 109–10
finishing (shellac and milk paint), 122–23
planning out parts, 105–6
preparing feet, 111
preparing for finishing, 115–16
preparing lid, 119–21
smoothing plane. *See* plane (smoothing)
spokeshave, projects using. *See* Perch Stool; Violin Knife
square, adjustable, projects using. *See* Hanging Wall Cabinet; 6-Board Chest
stop collar, using, 132, 135

thicknessing jig, 142

veneering and veneer press. *See* Hanging Wall Cabinet
Violin Knife, *11–21*
about: characteristics and uses, 11; sourcing wood blanks, 11; tools/materials and cut list, 12
gluing/clamping blade in place, 18
mortise for blade, 15–17
preparing wood blank, 13
refining shape, 20
shaping handle, 19
splitting blank in half, 13
using on other projects. *See* Album Crate; Dovetailed Box

Wooden Plane, *23–35*
about: blade and chip breaker, 23; overview of, 23; tools/materials and cut list, 24
break blank into parts, 26–28
create and install wedge, 32–33
drill out for pin, 31
finishing, 35
prep and cut parts, 25
put blank back together, 29–30
refine shape of plane, 34